UNDER CONSTRUCTION

GOD'S AT WORK

A Collection of Poems by Poet Ashley J

Credits

Published by TEAM PUBLICATIONS LLC
Brenda Hill, Editor-in-Chief
Champagne, Editor
Tracy Clark, General Manager Lake Charles, LA 70605

Text © 2019 by Poet Ashley J
www.poetashleyj.com

Cover Art © 2019 Leroy Tademy Jr.
Tademy Photography
www.tademydandp.com

Book Design: Vinh Alexander
www.vinhphotography.com

ISBN -13: 978-0-9969009-6-6

Printed in the United States of America
Published in the United States of America

Unless otherwise indicated, scripture quotations are from the King James Version of the Bible.

Library of Congress Cataloging-in-Publication Data
Johnson-Montegut, Ashley, 1990

Acknowledgements

April 2017, I published my first book, "Chains are Broken." Approximately two-and-a-half months after releasing my book, I experienced close loss for the very first time. It left me to press, pause and face the hardship that was on my mind. I did not feel the urge to write anymore. I felt empty. To be honest, I thought I was dreaming.

That day had to come eventually, I know. However, we are never really ready for death to show. I remembered that unfavorable phone call, when my grandma took her last breath. It was like my heart dropped in a huge puddle of sadness, leaving my face soaking wet. Thoughts were accumulating in my head. I was slightly angry and afraid. Quickly I realized God prepared me for this moment. He knew I believed that our relationship was strong enough that I could trust Him with any decision that He makes. See, I know Who heals, once someone breaks.

Naturally, mankind is selfish. We want what we want. If it was up to us, we would have our loved ones forever. However, I want to be unnatural. My grandmother was suffering and in pain on this side of life. God knew what was best for her. He gave her the new life she deserves. Often things happen, and we get annoyed, but the Bible says to count it all joy. Death does not have to be spooky. When I came to my senses and looked at things with a better eye, I began to see the beauty. Instead of being selfish, I choose to be selfless.

Twenty-six years I had the privilege to be in her presence and learn from her. I was blessed to be her granddaughter. She was able to witness my gift before passing. My grandmother's dream was to write. Unfortunately, the opportunity never presented itself to her, but God allowed it to live through me. God reminded me of this, and now I have put the pen to the paper again.

"Chains are Broken" released on time! She had the chance to read it before transitioning. I remembered her being so proud. Her words to me were, "You did a GOOD job!"

Even though she is not here to read this book or others to come, it still brings me joy to know she read that first one.

Contents

Chapter 4

Building The Foundation With Love...............81

Chapter 5

Electric Work...122

Chapter 6

The Black We Paint

Chapter 7

Living 2 Comfortable

To My Grandma, Lourine Magee

Chapter 1

Hard to Say Good-bye

To everything there is a season, and a time to every purpose under the heaven: A time to be born, and a time to die; a time to plant, and a time to pluck up what is planted;

--Ecclesiastes 3:1-2 KJV

Introduction

Life is funny, ain't it? Not funny as in "lol" or "kmsl." It is more like OMG IINOTIA (If it's not one thing, it's another). I know I am not alone. Sometimes life is like a butterfly that flies through beautiful seasons. However, there are those August 29th days where we are faced with natural disasters that turn our world into shambles. At times we may feel we need to be rejuvenated. In the beginning, God made us in the image of Him. Often times I wonder, "Did He really?" or, "Did He create us as a representation of a roller coaster that goes up and down in a dysfunctional circle?"

This is just my personal observation of mankind. When I take a quick look at others, my eyes reveal to me their confused and broken souls that want to be loved and/or longing for acceptance. From the view I am looking from, we look nothing like God. I see unforgiveness, division, and subtraction. We love, then we hate. We are real one minute, the next we are fake. At times, "Mankind" can be exhausting to deal with. It makes me think, "Is this why God rested after creating us?"

Maybe you've heard the phase, "You are a piece of work!" However, I like to believe, "We are a piece of art!" A masterpiece that is simply complicated, yet beautiful. Sometimes we are all over the canvas with different colors and crazy ideas, splashing our colorful feelings everywhere. Everyone cannot figure out the true image inside their creative painting, but there is always that someone who gets the picture. Who understands our creation better than the One who created us? God Only! Our Creator!

After pondering on my perception of people, I found it unfair to briefly examine man and throw us into just any basket. My discernment led me to scrutinize to make sure the details were clear as plastic. As I watched closely, I realized the true similarities between God and humanity. We both have intellect, emotion and will. So, YES! He designed us in His image.

What an honor it is to be chosen by God to be like Him. In order to know who we are, we first must know whose we are. It is essential to know who God is. Once we figure that out, there will be no room to be someone else because we are created by Him. The standard has been in position from the beginning. SO, STAY IN YOUR LANE. BE SET APART.

God is love, confirming we were created by love. Somewhere down the line we lost some of His finest characteristics, i.e., patience, devotion, integrity, wisdom, optimism, forgiveness, compassion and love. Now, we must map our way back to the image Our Creator created us in. It is time to start looking like Daddy again!

I pray you will discover a relatable message in these lines of my personal poems and allow God to upgrade you.

Let your curiosity detect your will to become brand new. Now the restoration may break you at first, but the result will be impeccable. Hold on because the renovation is necessary and your life will be under construction.

Within seconds of entering this world, we begin to die. It is only God who can permit us to rise.

It Will Be Alright

The last words that flowed from your lips
Before your eyes were permanently closed
Keep playing in my head
As if it was a catchy song on the radio

You said, "The road is going to be hard,
But it's going to be alright"
Then you went straight to praising God
There you left that night

It seems as if the pain had just left your body
And you were face to face with Him
The joy that came over you
Heaven, you must have seen a glimpse

You were tired
Ready to rest
But you waited for me and my sis to leave the hospital
And my mama and Tete (auntie) to fall asleep

To take your last breath

My eyes began to see the waterfall
Pouring down the stream of my disconnected face
My heart pounded
It raced
I chased after You God
Because You are the only One
Who can put my emotions back in place

For many of us
This is a hard pill to swallow
But I have to swallow it
Because I knew this day would eventually come
Where I would have to digest this fluid
The blood that left the veins of this family
Leaving us temporarily wounded
I just thank God wounds can be healed

For me to be able to still praise God
Even in my misery
Let me know that my grandma's spirit lives in me
Because that's what she did

She was a woman of strength
I never saw a tear

She kept it all together
Lord knows what all she held in

She was the rock
Not the one to break
Always kept it real
Did not see the need to be fake

She will tell you like it is
In such a polite way
I love this woman
That is why today we celebrate

This is not a funeral
This is more like the celebration of life
Funerals are for the dead
But my grandmother just received eternal life

I recognize that is the most important piece of this puzzle
Yes, we will miss our 'loss'
But she has gained
A new life in heaven
That was already proclaimed

I will remember all the things she has taught me
Like wear my best under clothes on Sundays

Walk with my head held high
Work for everything I want
And beg for nothing

The Lord is my Shepherd
I shall not want
I believe everything we need
He will provide
Even in this moment

In the honor of my grandma
I promise to stay with the Lord
I will go harder for God
Than ever before

All I want is to make you proud, Maw Maw
I know you always wanted to become a writer
But your dream was spiritually placed in me
I smile
Because now
Every time I write will remind me of how you
will always have a piece of me

I thank God I had the opportunity
Next step is to get to heaven
Where we can be one again

I won't allow anything to break this unity

Yes, I am in sorrow
Because you are my grandma
I am your granddaughter
But if I make this about me
How selfish will I be?
If I make this about me
How would I ever see what God is doing?

Yes, I am in sorrow
Because this is my grandma
But to her children
This is their mama
And I am sorry
Especially for my mama who dedicated her life to her

I can only imagine what you are going through
What you did for your mom
Believe I will do the same for you, Mama
I think my grandma would say, "Karen, be strong.
The road is going to be hard, but it's going to be alright.
Make me proud and hold on."

"I have been stored inside of Ashley.
She will be your rock and support.

You can finally live your life that you gave up for so long.
You have done your part by taking care of everyone,
putting yourself last, and everyone else first."

"Know that I am at peace.
No more will I suffer.
I will forever be your Mom
and you will forever be
My unforgettable daughter."

"Thank you for taking care of me!
But, it is time to live your life.
The road is going to be hard
But I promise, it will be alright"

My Tears

The moment I felt the water in my eyes
I knew why
I wish I could have held you longer
I wish I would have kissed every spot on your heart
to leave my mark
In remembrance of me

I wish I allowed every day to feel the sun
And every night to touch the moon
Instead, I blocked the rays that were coming through

Walking through life
Taking chances
Trying to catch every tear before it leaves
its common surface
All was not captured

I turned to God
If I am honest

I really want to blurt out every question that comes to mind
Like...What? How? Why?

My mama taught me not to question God
But every child feels they have a reason
The unknown brings complication to the grievin'
We cannot heal if we never begin the process of healin'

I have not been myself
I am ready to heal
Ready to feel normal again
I have been numb from the anesthesia

I began to sleep on life,
But it got real uncomfortable
Instead of resting on a pillow
I found myself sleeping on ice

It seems I could not move
I froze to the spot you left me
My heart was scarred
I felt the bruise

My tears are selfish
My tears are confused
My tears are sad

My tears have not yet been removed

My tears are weak
My tears are strong
My tears feel right
My tears feel wrong

My tears are my own
Dropping down my cheeks
My tears cry out to God
He understands my weeps

Tears I shed
But it is time to rest them
So, I grab the covers
To tuck them in bed

I miss your presence
I am slightly in denial
My body cannot digest this truth thoroughly
My flesh and spirit are in a rival

I am tired of being conflicted
I am tired of feeling like I am not winning
I am tired of sitting in this puddle
I am soaking wet

I am dripping

My tears are selfish
My tears are confused
My tears are sad
My tears have not yet been removed

My tears are weak
My tears are strong
My tears feel right
My tears feel wrong

My tears are my own
Dropping down my cheeks
My tears cry out to God
He understands my weeps

God dried up the wet land with His Son
I can go to Him for comfort
He is the One I lean on
When everything looks to go under

I am strong for the most part
In the flesh,
I am weak
I am always searching for strength

So, God I seek

The worry I must put down
Life is out of my control
I am learning to stay in my place
While God fulfills His role

Three in One Month

I really do not know how to articulate what I am feeling
Expressions are everything but expressed
Trippin' on inevitable things
I fell to less

Losing it all
I am starting to feel everything minus my best
I need a reality check

I do understand that obstacles are not always there
just to hold me back
I have to see the point of this test
So, I jump

I bump walls of obscurities
I am strong for the most part but I cannot front
Sometimes I get weak that my knees start to tremble
My eyes begin to get blurry
I cannot find my way out

I do not see the opportunity

I am blinded by my own eyes
I asked God to repair my vision
Replace it with something more spiritual
Remove the physical for it is useless
I need my sight to spot out what is visible in the
the storms of life

God let me clearly see You
Let me take delight in You
Because I know you will give me the desires of my heart
I believe that to be true

In this past month we lost a few
Grandma, in-laws
Life quickly turned into shambles

My heart is heavy
I am weighed down by catastrophe
Decorating my life with some kind of deadly confetti
And by the way,
I am not feeling this décor!

I must explore my options
Gotta stay open minded

Even though I really want to close the door
What will it solve?
Nothing at all

I must push
I fight every day and every night
With the thought of losing a piece of the family tree
It is really my selfishness
that wants you still here next to me

I check myself quickly
Realized it was your time
Nothing happens magically
God called you home
No lie
Anger tried to get the best of me

I am aware
Everything happens for a reason
This month my face got a taste of my salty teardrops
I witness my husband's pain
that naturally entered my veins
to share this connection

Tying the knots to capture something that feels sane
Because all of this is mentally driving us insane

Where is the umbrella?
There is way too much rain!

It is hard
Losing so much blood
I guess I should have built an ark
To prepare for the flood

Death is inevitable
Life is not guaranteed
That is why we must seek the intangible
Before we are broken down to our knees

God is the only One
Who can help us out of this puddle we are in
I refuse to drown
So, I begin to swim
Until the end

I am unsure of the depth of the pool
But I must go all in
Am I scared?
Of course!
But if I put my trust in Him
I know He will keep me safe

My heart aches
I feel like I cannot take anymore
I think I need a break
But wait,
What makes me so deserving of dodging
the bullet of suffering?

I am learning
I must go through it just like any other student
It is challenging
When this pain is speaking to me like it is fluent

What makes me weak makes me stronger
I was created to prosper
Cannot give up now
I am more than a conqueror

I am broken
But I am stronger than before
I have been chosen
No more will I ignore

I have been beat down
But the bruises do not define me
All is temporary
I am a royal soul

People cannot complete me
Only God can make me whole

So what am I tripping for?
Maybe it is time for me to move around
I got to start making movements
So, I am looking to You, God

Not at Loss

If you are wondering,
Are we alright down here?
Just know we are trying to make it
Without you this year

We have not really lost you
Because we know where you are
Sometimes we feel the pain of the open wound
But God heals the scars

I searched and found you in my dreams
When you visit me
I realize
I am not over you as it seems

I hide from the truth
Walls were built around me
Covering up reality
With a piece of excuse

I try not to visit your grave site too often
Because I feel I am not letting go
I want you to rest in peace
You would forever be with me
I do know

If I tell you it has been easy
Then the truth is not in me
I have yet to get over this cold
I need a spiritual remedy

A loved one like you
Is special to have
Your soul brought beauty to life
You are the art of every craft

You are my Angel
My light in dark places
As my story is being written
So far, you are the highlight on all the pages

We miss you dearly
Our heart is happy yet sad
Twisting our emotions
We cannot fully move forward
When we are stuck in the past

Sometimes our heart forms a hole
We are clumsy
So we trip
Falling more in love with the physical
rather than the soul

We focus on faces
Which is now missing from our view
We lost sight of the image of your soul
That painted the picture of the true you

I use to see you with open eyes
Now you are absent to my sight
I close my eyes to see you now
I can feel that everything is going to be alright

We are too small minded
To think outside the box
There are many ways to break free
We're just afraid to go through the blocks

Keep God in the mix
Every pain
Every brokenness
He can fix

There is a soul in the sky
We all can relate to
There is a spirit walking around
That we gravitate to

No more pain
No more suffering
We have to keep reminding ourselves
On this side of life
Nothing really seems fair

We ask ourselves why?
But everything is not for us to understand
God knows better than us
Just know
It was in His plan

Unforgettable You

Every day brings a thought of you
From the time the sun rises
In the early mornings
Until we can no longer see the morning dew

Memories green
But emotions turn blue
From the deep thoughts
Of not being able to see you

Facing reality is sometimes hard to do
But the inevitable does not take away
the constant thoughts
Of the sweet, loving, unforgettable you

Mental photos are the only thing that is left
So we must capture the poses
Place the memorable pictures in the album of our heart
Cherish the moments that is right underneath our noses

That we can smell, feel, taste, see, and touch

Breath is not really appreciated until we cannot breathe
What is life if we are not living?
Seeking a greater power than you and I
That has the capacity to let us see past the sky
Of our dark clouds we call pain
What is life if we never see the sun after the rain?

The day you left
It seemed gloomy, dark, cold, and lonely
It was a shadow blocking the light leaving a hole in our soul
We became hungry for you

As time passed
We realized the space you once owned
Never became vacant
You are forever with us
The love we have for each other will never be shaken

It was your vessel that left
But your spirit remains
With awe and amazement
That keeps lasting memories on our brain

I know you are here

From every thought and every tear
I close my eyes
And I can feel your presence

Every day brings a thought of you
From the time of sun rise
In the early mornings
Until we can no longer see the morning dew

Memories green
But emotions turn blue
From the deep thoughts
Of not being able to see you

Facing reality is sometimes hard to do
But the inevitable does not take away
the constant thoughts
Of the sweet, loving, unforgettable you

Beautiful as You

I want to see the beauty of every fruit
Have strength like roots
Planted deep down in grounds
Of everything that reminds me
You're beautiful

Still
Always will be the sun of days
The stars of night
Shining bright like 10 karats
Making my smile a daily uniform that I flaunt when I wear it

You make my heart beat like music
You make my mind question that which I am experiencing
Is it real or just an illusion?

Tuning in to the channel of love
Viewing wine that never ages so fine as you
You're beautiful

Looking through the pages of life
The hands of time move so fast
Before we know it
There goes a loved one
On the other side with Christ

We are forever trying to get it right
From all the bad mistakes
We make moves that are not moving us into a better place

We hold grudges
But we must get a grip
Hold tight to every fruit
Learn to take the bitter with the sweet
When you hear, "nothing is perfect"
Believe it to be true

Love should never go homeless
There are too many rooms to be filled
Shelter we must give
Prepare a place in our heart
And let love live

I want to see the beauty of every fruit
Have strength like roots

Planted deep down in grounds
Of everything that reminds me
You're beautiful

Inside and out
You glow like pregnancy
Giving birth to a beautiful legacy
You left behind to shine light that beams through darkness

Your beauty is defined
With words that describe your divine design
Heights I climb
Trying to get to your level
I have a long way to go
So get behind me you Ole devil

Sow Before You Go

I took a trip down to my memory
Where my thoughts traveled to this old scenery
There was fabric scattered all over
as if someone was about to start sewing
Putting material together seemed like it kept her going

It is something about the little things
Like her laugh
Her smile that put a personalized style to her face
I can still feel her hug as our arms embraced

See, we are so busy living for the moment
But I do not want a moment
Because that is too brief for me
I need something that will last like a good Ole memory
I want to relive the good times
shared for ten thousand centuries

Hand me a touch of peace

So I can remember how it feels
Show me love that is not mocked
So I can reminisce on something real

She left behind some fabric to help wipe away the grief
So we can pick up where she left off
And sow seeds that clothe us in love, comfort, and peace

Life calls us to do good deeds
Be there for one another, and teach
We have to be planters and sow the seed
But in order for us to grow together
We must feed

As family
We should stitch our heart together
So we can heal each other through this pain
If we allow God to cover us
Then we will be protected from the rain

Spring
Summer
Fall
Winter
God will catch us in our fall
Just holler, "Timber!"

Life experiences are for a reason
To everything there is a season
There is a time to be born, and a time to die
A time to smile, and a time to cry
If there is a time we get down, then know there will be a
time we will rise
There is nothing we cannot get through
When God is on our side

He realizes that life sometimes can leave us in
a poor mental state
He is aware when a loved one is taken away
It leaves the heart in ache
He knows that we do not always understand
the things we face
Even when we feel we do not need Him
He is always there, just in case

He will never leave us
Though we may feel alone
He will not forsake us
Even when things seem to go wrong

It is only God who can dry up this puddle
of tears that we are in
It is only God who can allow us to win in this season

They tell me
What we sow is what we reap
In this season let us sow unity so we can be united
Let us sow plentiful love where it can easily be divided
And shared among everyone who is in need of love
So we can be the ones to provide it

Let us make the most of life
While breath is still in our body
Sowing "the goods" should be our job
Instead of some type of hobby

Vigilance is required when we plant on this side of glory
Because one day someone will be reading our story

The best thing we can do for those that passed along
Is continue the legacy
Wipe our eyes, live to the fullest, and be strong

We must be ready for whatever life throws
Because tomorrow keeps no promises
So, sow before you go

Chapter 2

Home Improvement

What therefore God hath joined together, let no man put asunder.

--Mark 10:9 KJV

Take a good look inside your home. What have you observed? Is there unity, or does everyone get on each other's nerves? What type of interactions are going on? Have you ever felt like the house is full of people, yet you still feel alone? Are there several walls blocking the room to growth? Are relationships broken? Are mommy and daddy both available in the children's lives? Most importantly, is there God?

When I think about home, I imagine a personal place of comfort. A safe haven where we go for relief, to breathe, to escape from the world, and to be at peace. Home is more than a spot to lay our head; it is the address of rest and a shared space with loved ones.

Even though we may view our private domain as a comfortable, safe haven, the devil always invades. He will have husband and wives contemplating divorce, the fatherless feeling unworthy and considering suicide, families stop speaking to one another, and the list goes on. In those moments, we need God to shift some things around and make necessary home improvements.

It is important to get our house in order and let no man separate. We all can use a repair or two after the enemy has come in uninvited. Before the storms and hurricanes, it is vital that we stack our "faith funds" to get us through the process when the enemy comes.

Running Away My Company

My door is always open
Come in...
What do you really want from me?
You running away my company
What's this?

Assumptions jump to conclusions
What are we really doing?
I am so clueless

The invite is on the table
Cannot mail if there is no label
Is this working?
Or been disabled?
What's this?

My door is always open
Come in...
What do you really want from me?

You running away my company
What's this?

Do not be petty trying to clap back
Who is at fault for the set back?
Why so quiet when there is a question?
Saying nothing tells me something
Who does this?

The mirror is hard to look at
The reflection does not always come back
the way we want it
That is a fact
And opinions or just that

High in the air
Blowing mad wind will not change a thing
Together we can fly through any hurricane
If we trust God to be the pilot of this airplane

Get on board
Either you coming or you going
Either way I am already packed for it
Let me know
What it is

My door is always open
Come in...
What do you really want from me?
You running away my company
What's this?

Dark Night

The moon and stars
Are so far from tonight
Not a sparkle in the sky
It is way out of sight

I stumbled
Falling trying to reach
I must have hit my head
All I remembered was a sudden screech

Lying in my bed
Where I tossed and turned
Engaged in a pillow fight
Up from the nightmare
It is a dark, dark night

I cannot see
How did we get here?
Allowing space to divide us from getting near

I never thought
Love could be so dark
Bring back the light
Bring back the spark

The moon and stars
Are so far from tonight
Not a sparkle in the sky
It is way out of sight

Sleep is not the same without you
Love is not love
If I cannot share it with the one I love
What do I do?

A kiss means nothing
If it is not your lips pressed against mine
Let us go back into time
Where we were easily defined
Let us rewind

Tonight is black,
Clothes I pack
I trip like I ain't coming back

In the heat of the night

I write
Despite our fight
I continue to dream
Hoping that we might reunite

The moon and stars
Are so far from tonight
Not a sparkle in the sky
It is way out of sight

I want to view the moon again
And I want to see at least one star
I want to be wrapped in your arms
Protect me from the dark

Maybe my eyes are closed
Or I just cannot see the light
There is no moon
No stars
It is a dark, dark night

We Are Family

No matter what
Family is family
Blood
Adopted
Some extended the option
And blended two unions
We are blessed with different faces at the family reunion

We may not all resemble
The mirror gives us all a different reflection
But the one thing that should reflect the same is love
Shining through the dark alleys
Brightening up the darkest hour
Allowing us to lean on each other
To keep our heads above the puddle of tears
We are so close to drowning in

Days turn into night
And there we begin to fall asleep

In the darkness
We close our eyes
Only to dream of what it could be

Wake up
We have to stay prayed up
...weeping may endure for a night,
but joy cometh in the morning. Psalms 30:5 KJV

They say, "A family that prays together stays together"
So my hands meet
Lifting my request to God
Because this world will tear us apart if we let it
Only God can unwrap us, from the arms of destruction
You can bet it

I believe family is missing that "back-in-the-day-love"
That "let-nothing-separate-you-love"
That love
That love where disagreements won't cause
unnecessary bridges
We rather go a mile
When it only requires some inches
Every wound does not require stiches

Some just need a simple touch

Or a quick check up
Let that person know you are praying for them
And you are here if they need you
But somewhere we have lost touch

I am slightly bothered
I guess you can say I am in my feelings a little bit
I am feeling some type of way
Because technology is a snake
Sneaking around to take away the meaning of relationships

Technology gives an avenue
For families to drive right through
without verbalizing a greeting
Going through the whole day
without checking up on one another before the evening

I am mad at technology because it took away our voice
Leaving us mute
It is sad
Because if the internet crashes
Some would not know what to do

To our family that is right in front of our eyes
It seems we turn to ice
Giving them the cold shoulder

While our eyes are glued to our mobile device

The people that is right next to us
We avoid
And wonder why so many relationships are being destroyed
We are too busy trying to get likes
from people that do not necessarily like us despite

It is all about capturing the moment
While missing out on the moment
The moment where we can talk face to face
Sit back and reminisce on old memories
Laughing at stories told
Because some stories are so unbelievable

We must cherish every second together
The time will come when your loved one will be no more
You do not want to live with regrets
Thinking of all the shoulda, woulda, coulda
Because you chose to ignore

Family is not just something we are born into
It is something that is created
I do not want technological love
I want destiny
Something that has already been activated

Family I can count on
So family I seek
Family is that treasure that is most important to me

When I am broken
They help mend me to make me whole again
With their inspiring words and expeditious actions
Quickly they gather up all my pieces
One by one
The amazement leaves me speechless

Family is always there
When one is down
Reach and help them up
Each other's burdens we should bear

We will fuss and fight
Experience many calamities
But at the end of the day
Remember,
We are family

Family Over Everything

Have you ever found yourself soaking in a tub of
depression?
Leaving your mind at the thought of suicide
Have you ever felt the pain of abandonment?
Because your parents showed no effort to make an effort

Mama too busy looking for you a new daddy
Because daddy is nowhere to be found
You are a lost child
Trying to figure out everything on your own
While noise is playing loud in your head
There you struggle to turn down the sound

Thoughts are a musical
Do you hear the instruments making classical beats?
Nothing is new under the sun
It is the same old thing
History repeats

The right path gets hard to follow
Have you ever felt like giving up
because the pill just got too big to swallow?

Have you ever felt rejected?
Have you ever felt disrespected?
Have you ever just stopped and listened to your heart beat?
Are you afraid that your life is slightly oblique?

We cannot choose family
So we must make the best with what we have
Sometimes we get disconnected from the laughs
But just hold on
Life is a test
And we must pass the class

Family,
We ride for 'em
We "die" for 'em
But most of all go to God for 'em

We have to let go and let God
The fight gets hard sometimes in the ring
But we do what we have to
That is what we call
Family over everything

Sleep Depression Sleep

Does He love me?
Am I good enough?
Does He even care if I exist?
A list of questions a child may ask
When dad is missed

Falling in deep waters of depression
The panic attacks begin
Hoping not to drown in dejection
And leaving life to end

Sleep depression sleep
God wake them up from this anxiety
Children are dying from lack of happiness
A black room they find themselves in
Screaming for help
"Parents are you listenin?"

Can't eat

Can't sleep
Suicidal thoughts
Depression
Anxiety

So much is on their mind
From the things they face in today's society
Are we ignoring the scattered pieces?
Or, looking at the puzzle in its entirety?

Do we pray for them?
Every time they step foot into this world;
are we asking God for coverage
to protect these boys and girls?

Lucifer keeps it poppin'
He ain't stoppin'
He is always on his job
Destroying
Causing confusion
Compulsive lying

So that is where we clock in
and work overtime
It pays to shower with love
Like every day is Valentine's

These kids are seeking for love
Some will find it in places that are corrupt
Get to their heart
Before the streets snatch them up

The youth need you present
As you can see
Child support does not give them stability
It means nothing if you do not give them time
when you have the availability

These kids need you to show up and be active
Keep them safe
They need someone who is protective

Mothers, I hate to tell you
But buying love will not make them happy
Gifts do not make up for the guilt of falling for the wrong man
They are forced to call daddy

Not trying to be rootless
Just letting you know what the truth is
They want peace
Without everybody chunking up the deuces

Nobody got time for 'em

Everyone is too busy
Living their own life
Tossing these kids around
And wonder why they are so dizzy

When was the last time you insured them of their value,
answered their questions
and let them know they are loved?
More beautiful than a dove
They are more than good enough
And yes, you care that they exist
Why have the opportunities to confess your love and still
resist?

So many ideas of the youth
People believe they should be problem free
They think kids have no worries at all
But the bible says, "Even the youths shall faint and
be weary, and the young men shall utterly fall:" Isaiah 40:30
KJV

Kids get tired of being part of the fatherless
Being bullied
Pressured by peers
Feeling like they do not fit in
Always feeling lost because they have yet to sense the win

To parents,
Listen to them
Be more available
Make it comfortable for your child to come to you
Even when it seems uncomfortable

Introduce them to God
So they can meet someone who is bigger than that bully
Bigger than anything they may face
He will give them the power to knock down fear with faith
And then, anything they will be able to embrace

To the youth,
Turn to God
He can fight battles for you

Do not be afraid to stand out
God did not create you to fit in
The devil is trying to trick you with his smooth lies
and make you feel you are losing
This season is your season to win

Still Love You

When I was a little girl
My daddy was there
Until my mama got tired
And he left
Now I cannot find him anywhere

When I got older
I realized he was never present to begin with
I saw him in a light that seemed different

I became aware of his spirit was never there
It was just his body
Not active in my life
Too full of stuff that brings you to the potty

A father figure, He has yet to figure it out
With all those failed promises
Why tell a lie?

I do not know what that is about

I cannot live my life holding on
The weight has become too heavy
My hands are now sweaty
Slipping off of you
I let go
Because there was nothing left for me to do

Even in the pain
Daddy, I still love you
I know you are thinking,
"You love me?"
"I am unworthy"
"Love is earned, and I have not earned it"
No, daddy that will be trust
Love is giving, the day it becomes you
It becomes me
It becomes us

Love is long suffering
How can I determine I suffered long enough?
I will not close my heart
Because God does not give up on us
But your absence will not continue to consume me
I will be right here if you ever decide you ready to do your part

I am ready to move forward
It is no way I will let the past pass me up
I and it cannot be on the same level

I have graduated
To motivated
Dedicated to continue to be elevated
Fear stops the growth
It seems my soul got tied to yours with a tight rope
But I cut it
Freedom I wrote

I found my oxygen
As I was packing up to move
Ran across some unopened packages
That I wished I would have fully accepted
As soon as it was delivered

I should have listened, when I was spoken to
But stubbornness was all in my routine
Until I became all ears to *Ephesians 4:18 KJV*
Having the understanding darkened,
being alienated from the life of God through
the ignorance that is in them,
because of the blindness of their heart:

That verse opened my eyes
I was living like the gentiles
But no longer
It was just separating me from the life of God
No longer
I want to be closer

I will not say you left my heart hard
I am the one who made that choice
Cannot play the blame game
without taking some aim
Being real with myself
Help cleanse my soul
Now I can rejoice

I want my understandings to have light
Cannot separate from the life of God
I need Him
When things are easy
And when things get tight

I want to be forgiven for my sins
So I must forgive you
Time is expiring
Time to pay what is due
Cannot imagine what it is like

If you never walked in those shoes
It is a reason you were not there
But yet,
It is still no excuse

Chapter 3

Blueprint

I will praise thee; for I am fearfully and wonderfully made: marvelous are thy works; and that my soul knoweth right well.

--Psalms 139:14 KJV

W oooooow!! This blueprint is so to die for! The way God designed us is beyond gorgeous! We should be in awe of God and have "mad respect" for His power.

The way God created us with great depth and thoughtfulness shows His passion and creative capabilities. If we take a good look inside and see what we are truly made of, we can appreciate our life and God more. It will be easier to demolish every surface that prevents us from standing firm on the word of God. We would not worry about fitting in to something that never had room for us to begin with. We would accept who and whose we are.

Our Father loved us so much. When we were on the verge of dying, God gave His only Son because He thought we were worth saving. He sees value in us that we may not see in ourselves

Dad made us the salt of the earth. In every season, I believe He wants us to give life flavor, but sometimes we are so bland and distasteful. We all have something to offer but so many are just going through the motion. Instead of having our eyes on Jesus, the true standard, we have our eyes on each other. We give too much power to people that hold us down and make us feel valueless.

Own who you are and walk in your greatness. God created us all the same with different exterior without accident. Not one is perfect. We all get wounded. However, the God of miracles gives us His beauty for our ashes. What a trade! We should praise thee for we are fearfully and wonderfully made!

I Am Not That Chick

I am not that chick you can downgrade
No disrespect
You are not of any interest to me
We do not even fit
You are way too dim
I am lit

Here is some shade
Erase that fantasy in your head
You cannot get me in bed unless you marry me

Oh wait... Paul already popped the question
So you can X me
I know I was your target
But sorry
Ashley is off the market
But there you go

Would not stop trying

Even after I told you I am married
You turn around and ask me,
"Is it happily?"
Why?

I guess you think you can do better
Come on, bruh
I will hit you with some cold words
Make you wanna grab your sweater

I am reading your persona,
I know your type from a distance
Spitting deathly lines like,
"I will sweep you off your feet until you are unconscious."
Boy that is called a coma
Move around before I hurt your feelings
I really don't wanna

I am a Christian
But you about to make me do this
I am about to withdraw
Just call me a debit
Hold up, before I lose my religion
Here is the door
You go

Just in case you could not find the exit
Next girl you encounter
Make sure you fix yourself
Your whole approach needs to be edited

What is going on in your brain?
Check your head
You must be sick
If you think my marriage will be disrespectful
Boy bye,
I am not that chick

I Am Not That Woman

I am not that woman who needs you to be defined
You cannot boost my esteem with your corny lines
And you sure cannot tear me down
Leaving my face with a frown

See,
I know who I am
Confidence is all mine
There is a well that never runs dry
So I drink until I am filled
with the blood of the Son of Man,
who was crucified
I eat the fruit as it comes
I just want to be satisfied

What I eat, drink or wear
Is not my worry
I know God will supply
He is always there

So I know I can rely

I am a daddy's girl
A King's daughter
Strong enough to hold my own
Wise enough to kneel to the throne
Intelligent to know

I am more than a Negro

I am a royal soul
Wonderfully made and not afraid
I stand bold
With my chest out
Arms are folded
Yes I am sassy
But so

Does my sassiness upset you,
as it dances the night away?
Does my confidence make you feel small,
when I say thank you to the ugly things you say?

You may think you are higher than me
But you can dismount
I am equally worthy

Keep your coupon
I do not accept any discounts

Tear me down
Belittle me
Go ahead and try
I come up from a knock down
Because my strength falls from the sky

Recreated

Looking back on my birth certificate
I remembered reading it to apprehend
the moment I was born
Placed into life to adorn

I put my touch on the world
Not sure how beautiful I have made it
God took His time with my creation
But I am positive I made a mess out of what He has created

It seems to be one thing after another
It never fails
But it is good to know Jesus,
who can get us out this hell

October 2008
The Lord took me back into His custody to recreate
The time was looking right
So I went into the water to gain new insight

Stepped out and I felt naked, clean
I felt free
The weight was lifted off my shoulders
But I knew the enemy was coming closer,
on my new journey
Trying to get me to surrender
So, I shielded my soul with every bible verse
I could remember

I asked God to never leave me
As always
By request
He delivers

If you ask you will receive
I realized that birth certificate was dated wrong
I felt I was being deceived
I believed I was living
But I was breathing a lie all this time
And the only way to get over it,
I had to climb

I recalled being in war with myself
Without the proper tools to fight
I remember my thoughts
Were darker than midnight

The evidence of hate that was given to me
I stored it in my heart
How was I living
when everything around me was falling apart?

I've been recreated
With a spirit that is sturdy
Made from dirt
But I am not as "dirty"

My truth is
I am nowhere near perfect
At times, I struggle to lift others up
Because inside I am hurtin'

My truth is
Naturally, I sin
Thankfully I am saved by grace
A gift that helps me to win

My truth is
I love God because He loved me first
He captured my attention
Opened my eyes to help me see
No one has my back
He is the only One who can save me

I stepped into this world dying
Because I did not know the truth
God I know now
Birth is life inside of You

We should thank God for the re-creation,
A second chance is a privilege we fail to give ourselves
But I am chosen life without the expiration
I want the story without the tales

It seems to be one thing after another
It never fails
But it is good to know Jesus,
Who can get us out of this hell

The Way You See Me

Do you know who you are?
Behind the shades are many spaces
There you hide your greatness
Seeking for approval in all the wrong places
And minimizing your worth

Ye are the salt of the earth.
Matthew 5:13 KJV

Ye are all children of light, and the children of the day:
we are not of the night, nor of darkness.
1Thessalonians 5:5 KJV

But ye are a chosen generation, a royal priesthood,
a holy nation, a peculiar people;
that ye should shew forth the praises of him
who hath called you out of darkness into his marvelous light.
1 Peter 2:9 KJV

For we are his workmanship,
created in Christ Jesus unto good works,
which God hath before ordained that we should walk in them.
Ephesians 2:10 KJV

You are fearfully and wonderfully made.
Psalms 139:14 KJV

God sees us
Differently than we view ourselves
We look out of eyes that are brutal
Seeking for approval
We look through eyes of pain, betrayal, hurt and
and rejection
Leaving us in search of love, loyalty and perfection
Trying to connect in a way
that nothing will hinder our connection

The world forms all types of opinions
But it really doesn't make a difference
Because now, I know who I am

I am a King's daughter
I am a royal soul
I am precious and free
I break off strongholds

I was in the world
Giving in to the temptation
But I been born again
I am a new creation

I am created by righteous and holy
I have not just been called
I am chosen
I am designed for good works
I am preparing for my promotion

I know who I am,
Because I know who You are
You Are "I Am Who I Say I Am"

God defined me
Before the world laid its imperfect, judgmental eyes on me
God labeled me as His child
Those weapons of your evil words will not prosper
Sometimes we must stay still for a little while

I am love
I am powerful
I am beauty from above

I am light
Shining through heavy hearts
I am holding tight to the arts
The picture
You painted from the start
Is the only image that captures my attention
I am delivered from my past
Just call me redemption

I been saved
By amazing Grace
The perfect gift You gave
To help me finish this race

I am whatever You say I am
I will not listen to the voice of man
To place me in a category they think I should stand

I am not interested in their thoughts of me
They only focus on my ashes
But You see my beauty
Me, You have fully examined
So the way You see me is the way that I am

My Make-up Is My Wakeup

I believe I am always beautiful
Ok... Except in the mornings when I wake from my sleep
And the cold flood my eyes
So much I can barely see

See, a lot of women get up
Instantly preparing for the day
Some put on make-up
So they would not step out any kind of way

I do the same but my make-up is slightly unique
Instead of blending in
I let my in bring me out
Using a spiritual technique

No blush
No coffee in my cup
All I need is another day
Just to get me up

My make-up is the morning sun
Shining through the window
Making my eyes pop
A sign that signals my day
has the perfect intro

My make-up is my wake up
First thanking God for today
His grace brings a coat of love
That brightens my face

Sometimes I notice when something is missing
I apply my smile
To bring out that joy to show
I am happy to be living

My smile brings the blush
That old concealer was hiding my best part
Down the toilet
I flush
Call it blemish,
I call it spark

I mess up when I rush
God fix it with Grace powder
Mercy He showers

Negativity I brush

How can I frown?
Blessings run over in my cup
I won't be down
He keeps me up

I salute with a kiss
My lip sticks to Him
Showing appreciation
For all those times
He went out on a limb

He is my foundation,
When all hope is gone
Unlike the serpent,
I actually have something to stand on

Who I am has been ordained
God made my blue print
So, He is the only One who can claim
I am His prized possession
Just stamp "God's Property"
next to my name

I put on Jesus
Then I know my light will shine
He gives me peace
Even in destruction
I want to be comfortable enough to recline

No blush
No coffee in my cup
All I need is another day
Just to get me up

Grace is what makes me gorgeous
Forgiveness is the reason I look so flawless
Those thorns Jesus wore,
Reminds me I am to die for

Compassion compliments my heart
Love sexy up my thoughts
My make-up comes from above
God gave me definition
So, I know what I am made of

No blush
No coffee in my cup
All I need is another day
Just to get me up

My make-up is my wake up
What you see is what you get,
I am enough
If you cannot stand me,
Then you are welcome to sit

Chapter 4

Building The Foundation With Love

*And now abideth faith, hope, charity, these three;
but the greatest of these is charity.*

--1 Corinthians 13:13 KJV

L ife is an option, but love is a command. I have noticed that when my husband and I get into fights, sometimes things get out of hand. Arguments can last longer than it should. At times, we invite yesterday's drama into our present day. However, we are learning that we must build our foundation on love and let nothing stand in our way.

Authorize love to get in between a relationship of "I and U." (ILOVEU) Unhidden love covers a multitude of dilemmas. It exposes the beauty of each other's flaws. This great emotion makes tough times less painful. It allows for confronting moments to be less offensive. It is important that we do and say everything out of love.

Love is the biggest four letter word I know. Love is an action word we must show. God demonstrated an amazingly beautiful love for us to have. He so loved the world that He gave His only Son. Some people have more than two sons and could not imagine giving up either one.

Created in the image of God, have adoration for each other like Him. Every thought we think, should be based on that big four letter word. If love is not on the brain, then what is? It is time to change our heart and our mind. Build everything on love so we can better exemplify God.

What Is Love?

The day my niece pops the question....
"What is love? ....

This is what I will tell her:
Love is patient
Love is kind
Love is deeper
Than our mind
Love...

I will try to explain it in the simplest terms
I know how, so you can understand
Love is when you like a person a lot, a lot
And you always want them near
You know that feeling you have for your family
Like mommy and daddy and TETE (auntie) that is
unexplainable?
That is love
Born at birth,

An incredible emotion that is undeniable

Love is what your heart forms on paper
Love are things that brings you unexpected smiles
Like candy that is not really good for your teeth,
but it is something about the flavor
Love is a big deal
Love is major

After the rain, it brings a rainbow in the sky
Displaying all sorts of colors
Like red, orange, yellow, green, blue, indigo and violet
Love does not need loud painted words
to make the heart vibrant
It speaks volume on its own
You can hear it when the universe is silent

Love is that little feeling
that tingles in your soul
Love is so powerful
Turns brown days into gold

Besides oxygen,
Love is one thing we cannot live without
It is worth going out of space to chase
Because that life, love is about

Love makes you go wild
But love sits you still
Love is always in style
Love is so real

Love is hot
Love is chill
Love is everything
It cannot be touched,
but you can definitely feel

Love does not tear down
It is there to build
Love is the best emotion expressed
Love covers a multitude of sin
It cleans up life's messes

Love is an action word
It brings the phrase "I love you" to existence
Sometimes space gets in between
Only to make room for love
to travel a greater distance

Sorry I got so deep
But love is profound
It takes you places unimaginable

Love blows your mind

Love makes you full of words
Love makes you speechless
Love knows your strength
Love knows your weakness

Love causes no harm
It is innocent like you
Pure and sweet
So, so beautiful

It is everything you can think of
And I want you to fully experience it,
My love

A Mother

It is something special about a mother
Especially the ones that do not have any help
Carrying all the weight all by themselves

She grows tired and weary
But she does what she has to do
She gets down and out
Sometimes she is blue

She does not stop when she needs to go
She does not give up when she feels there is no hope
She goes to God
She understands life is no joke

What is a mother if she did not care?
What is a mother if she never was there?
A mother is the backbone of the family
A mother sometimes plays the role of mommy and daddy

A mother,
She brings life to the universe
Putting herself last and everyone else first
She is unstoppable

Woman is one of the most beautiful creations
The way God designed woman
I can understand man's temptations

Her body is art that changes in time
Even with the marks, the crease
Her body is still a masterpiece

Her body is paint giving life to the canvas
She has softness about her
that gives others chances after chances
She is promising
Every spot of her is astonishing

She gives light to the world
Populating it to fill the void
Without woman, earth would be left empty
Like those two cities God destroyed

It is no way a man can carry that type of weight
Just the sight of birth makes some men faint

God knew for man to bring in life, just was not meant
Because they are not as strong as woman

Oh how amazing is she
There are only a few things woman cannot do
What man does with ten different hands,
woman does it with two

You are strength that cannot be measured
You are a miracle worker
Giving water to the desert
Eyes have not seen all you do on the regular
You are every character on stage
Playing every role to pick up the slack
for those who were not brave

You paid the way for the next generation
Teaching them all you know through your actions
Trying to give them a clear illustration
of what showing up looks like
So they won't draw to the absence

You put beauty in beautiful
No one can compare to you Mother
God created you different than man for a reason
He knew you were the right seed that can blossom

in every season

You adjust well to circumstances
Your finances may not be all the way there
But you make do with what you have

You are no secret
People just do not see all the cards on the table
God sees,
You are an Angel

Mother,
You are God chosen
There is no one like you
You are strong
You are powerful
But most of all
You are simply beautiful

My Everything

My heart beats
With the extension of gravity
of your love
My heart beats
With ease of air
that precisely collaborates with my lungs
You are my everything
All I ever dreamed of

You are my rays of sun
My island breeze
The sweet aroma to my nostrils
The fruit of my tree

Build me up
Encourage me
Hold tight to my body
Love me

You are my everything
All I ever dreamed of
You are a blessing
A gift from up above

His Rib

There are three functions of the ribs:
Protection
Support
Respiration

God performed an operation,
Took man and created a woman
From one of man's ribs

They count on each other to properly breathe
Cannot afford to be in separation,
When one became two
Those two became one
Joined together in celebration

His rib is the function of her being
He is protective, supportive and he gives her air to breathe,
When she feels she is running out of breath
From those long days of taking care of everyone

and everything in her presence

But yet,
She does not regret
Because she has her rib
whose love is attached to the essence
of her strength
Holding her down from everything she's up against

Man leads
Without Adam there is no Eve
Everything goes together
Like fruit to a tree

His rib would never be in existence
If God did not take the time
To form him from the dust of the ground
And breathed into his nostrils the breath of life
When he went into that deep sleep

Waking up to his companion
Without thinking twice
He instantly sees his woman
Equally beautiful as life

Bone of his bone

Flesh of his flesh,
From the operation
He had to be impressed

Before she
He was lonely
In the Garden of Eden
Looking for a help mate
God sent him birds
And all other living creatures
But nothing as great as his rib

Those other lives were becoming
But had nothing on his woman
What is the greatest gift?
When life you give

It is better than money, car or a crib
See, woman would not exist without man
But man is incomplete without his rib

His Queen

A bond shared between man and wife
Never should it be broken,
You may argue and fight
But remember the vows once spoken

Marriage is a full-time job
100 percent you both shall bring,
Leave no room for space
Breaks are for the spring

King adores his queen
His vision is clear to see her beauty from afar,
He has the power to heal
Every spot where she has been scarred

For his queen
He puts "I love you" to action,
Understanding that "I love you" is not just an expression

He recognizes her royalty
She is his prized possession
He values her presence
Like she is the best thing sent from heaven

Queen submit to your king
King love your queen
Like Christ loved the church
And He gave his life for it

Every day will not be filled with roses
Every day will not be filled with thorns
Some days may be gloomy
Find light in that moment
Again, you will experience marriage beauty

For better or worse
Through thick and thin
No matter what
Be down for the win

When God Created You

When God created you
He made you special,
He took caution
He took his time
Because he knew you would be for me
Even when I did not know you would be mine

He knew for you to deal with me would take some time
So He made you patience

When God created you
He designed you to give my life purpose
He made you that light bulb
Giving light to every dark room in my life
He knew you were the man for me
So he blessed me to be your wife

I love every ounce of you
Your soul,

Your spirit is so beautiful

Every day with you is a blessing
I am constantly learning
Every day teaches new lessons

I am thankful to call you my husband of 6 years
We experienced joy
We also shared tears
Together we embrace whatever appears

Forever is inevitable
No gift can compare to your presence
To be without you is unimaginable,
I want to spend the rest of my life with you

You are my soul mate
To be without you
My soul would ache
In pain every day
My sky would be full of rain

You bring the sunshine
I am glad I took your last name and placed it against mine
You and I are a masterpiece that shines
And deserves to be placed inside of a frame

Eternity with you I claim

I love you more today than I did yesterday
But tomorrow I will love you even more
Every second with you is another moment
I adore and enthuse to explore

Thank you for being you
Nothing less
Nothing more
Happy Anniversary
And let us continue to soar
I love you

Let Love, Love on You

I am not the one who hurt you
There is no reason for your heart to be guarded
Please leave room for me to enter
Do not be so cold-hearted

Let love, love on you
Passionately
Oh so gentle

Kisses of the truth
of why I really fell in love with you
Hugging on the root of this relationship
It started when we were just a youth
Chocolate, brown brother
There is no one like you

Let love, love on you
Passionately
Oh so gentle

I see the moon and stars
When I look into your eyes
When I am around you,
I am like a fat child at a concession
Doggone it I am in heaven

I love you
Even with all your imperfections;
There is no one like you

Let love, love on you
Passionately
Oh so gentle

Hold me in your strong arms
And never let me go
I will be here regardless
To feel a spirit so gorgeous
You give me the perfect beam
Even in my darkness

I am in love with your patience
Waiting without rush
The crush you had on me in the beginning
I crushed
But trust

Being with you is a must

I cannot live a day without you
Or maybe I can
But I really do not want to
With you is where I want to stand

So let love, love on you
Passionately
Oh so gentle

I felt the butterflies
When God sent me you
I still get those feelings
Every minute we get close
You give me healings,
Headaches,
Passion,
Love
And all other types of deep feelings

You give me sun after the rain,
You give me joy after the pain,
You give me hope when I give up,
You love me like Christ loves the church
See, that's what's up

You are my right-hand man
Sometimes I cannot stand you though,
And I ain't playin'
I am telling the truth
But it is just once in a while,
Every blue moon

We go through ups and downs
Just like every marriage,
But we experience more ups
The connection we have is different than the average

You are actually my best friend
We fuss
We fight
But love always wins
It is God
The reason why we are this amazing union

I give Him all the praise
And I am not just saying this to say the same old phrase
that most Christians say
I mean it
I do not want to watch the same old episode from my past,
I've already seen it

Where He brought me from
When He brought me through,
He sent me to you

He knew you would give me what I was missing,
Not so you can complete me
Because when He created me,
I was already complete

Somewhere down the road we fall
And get scratches and bruises
You are my cupid
Catching me in my fall to place bandages on every spot
I have been wounded

I just want to return the favor
If you were Jesus,
I would call you my Savior
But since you are not
I will just call you later

To marinate love all in your body, soul
and deep off in your mental
So you can let love, love on you
Passionately
Oh so gentle

My Whole Life I Waited for You

I have waited my whole life for you
As I stumbled over many mistakes
In search of you

I kept missing
The beauty of true love
Blindfolded by the world,
I could not clearly see who is above

My Lord, I wanted my significant other so bad
That I eagerly sat in the pulse of anticipation,
Hoping to receive my personalized package
That You have specifically detailed with perfection

My soul mate
A spiritual connection was meant to be connected
It is destiny,
If it's all good
It's all God

Father is the only
One who knows what is best for me
So, I have waited on Him this time

My priorities were scrambled
He was always in the mix,
Honestly, not always my first pick
But now he is forever it

I let go of all the control
Because I was losing
Truly I really did not have it to begin with

I had to learn to be patient,
Not rushing for that man to find this woman
He created so caringly and adorably
The being and meaning of husband and wife is lovable

Before I knew you
I was already making sacrifices to make room for you
I could not have you when I first wanted to
Because my life was cluttered
So I began to fast and pray,
Pray and fast,
Got rid of some things now here I am
Living out the dream where

Prince Charming meets his Madame

I take your hand
Only to hold it close to mine,
Locking fingers
Only to find there is no separation

Where I blossom,
You blossom
Where you fall
I will be right there to help you up,
Vice versa
Two are now one
I will proudly sign your name at the end of mine,
I will ink it in cursive

We are not the average signature,
We are heavenly chosen
The best thing that was laid out on the surface
It was God who brought me to you
The bridegroom has found his bride
The search is due

She is the King's daughter
He is the King's son
This day we marry

For better or worse
Til death do us part

Today is confirmation
Two is now one

Amazing Soul that Came to Life

I pray that every day you see the reason why
God brought this prince to you
And every day you see the stars and the moon,
I pray the moon and stars
are just as beautiful up close as it is afar

Let love get personal
Creating magical bliss
From even the most simplest,
And gentlest kiss

Divorce is not really optional
Marriage is a connection of love that is exceptional,
Cannot really live without it
It is the greatest commandment
So follow the demands given and love
While love, loves on you

The prince has met his princess
Only to make her queen
He sees the value of woman
Royal is she

He is the only candy in her eye
To him she is the most amazing soul that came to life
So he captured this beautiful butterfly to make her his wife
Because she is the most amazing soul that came to life

No more searching for his rib
Because there she is
No more traveling the world to look for his wife
He has found his better half
The most amazing soul that came to life

Who knew how far across the world was the adventure
To get to the prize God has delivered
A package designed so specific

Some do not get a chance
To find their romance
But this prince found his woman

I pray that every day peace will live in you
And everyday you both see marriage

at its greatest value

Let love get personal
Creating magical bliss
From even the most simplest,
And gentlest kiss

See the prince has met his princess
Only to make her queen
He sees the value of woman
Royal is she

He is the only candy in her eye
To him she is the most amazing soul that came to life
So he captured this beautiful butterfly to make her his wife
Because she is the most amazing soul that came to life

Angelic Kiss

I know Jesus is alive
Because I see Him when I smile
In the presence of the mirror I glance
And there is the reflection of His crown

The deeper the cuts
The more I am aware of His blood,
I am dodging the fire
Just as Noah built an ark to prepare for the flood

The walls are falling
Improperly built
The foundation is weak
First it stands
Next it slips

I am in need of Your angelic kiss
Gentle lips
Against my chest

Caressing the pain
With Your holiness

Obstacles stand in the way
I reach for You
But the breakable wall
I built with stubbornness
Caused me to be attached to something that is not of You

Pretending to have a hard shell
Eyes were clearly laid on me
You are able to see right through

I am in need of Your angelic kiss
Gentle lips
Against my chest
Caressing the pain
With Your holiness

Your purity cleansed me
Your grace sustains
The bumps and bruises scarred me
But did not destroy me

It was all in vain
When all is temporary

You remain

I am healed
By Your stripes
By Your fight
By Your Spirit
By Your lips

I am in need of Your angelic kiss
Gentle lips
Against my chest
Caressing the pain
With Your holiness

I am in need of You
I need Your love to remove the hate
I need Your truth to cast out the fake
I need Your touch
So I can feel something different than a heartbreak

I need Your strength to move me
I need Your power for electricity
Give me light to know when I am in darkness
Let me be aware of all Your creativity

Moving mountains

Hiking hills
Climbing cliffs
Reaching for You
I need an extra lift

Give me Your lips
I am in need of Your angelic kiss
Gentle lips
Against my chest
Caressing the pain
With Your holiness

Te amo mucho (I Love You So Much)

Jesus,

I am sorry for what You had to go through

That crown of thorn

Being pierced on Your side

Died on that cross

Is more of a reason why I love You

The word tells me that love is patient

Love is kind

You show me how deep is Your love

And I will show You mine

Te amo mucho is the deepest,

Most romantic love in the Spanish language

And that is the type of love I have for you

Jesus,

I love you

A leader

I am proud to follow

Righteous You are
In my soul,
There was left a hallow
Until I accepted You in my life
At first,
In my eyes,
Your presence was a pill that was hard to swallow

I admit
Before, I denied You
Immaturity caused the neglection
I was not scared of death
I thought I had all I needed for protection

I was a fool using tools that broke bonds
Leaving distance,
A space between You and I
From the bars I put up that was made of iron

I treated You as if
You were the average guy that shattered my heart
From the failed promises and lies
I now realize
You are not that guy
You are Jesus,
The son of the Living God

To know love Is to know God
For God is love
And You are just like your Daddy

Sins I commit
But He cast it into the depths of the sea
He is forgiving

I am sorry
I did not always love You
I lied with my mouth and said I did
I was not really showing You
How honest was my truth?
How long did it have to take?
For me to see right before my face,
A Man of Grace
Lord have mercy on my soul!

You have filled the space that was once empty
The world offered me so much
But I was still incomplete
I always felt there was something else missing
I was without You
And I no longer want to be

I thank God for You

Jesus, now I am complete
And I am for sure that I love You
I know You love me

Jesus,
I cannot express in all words
Of how much You mean to me
It is far past my vocabulary
No dictionary
has the exact words to define You
Awesome is good
But even that word is like an insult to You
You are so much more than incredible

Since I cannot find the words
I will let my actions speak
I am not a songstress
But best believe my notes will be on key
Proudly walking in the door that
Our Father has allowed to open just for me
I love Your spirit that has been stored inside of me

Te amo mucho(I love you so much)
Indeed Lo eres todo (You are everything)
And that I do mean

You are my inspiration
The light of my day
You are my Savior
Protecting me from all harm
You are my Comforter
Holding me gently in Your arms

Jesus,
I said it before
I cannot express in all words
Of how much You mean to me
It is far past my vocabulary
No dictionary
has the exact word to define You
Awesome is good
But even that word is like an insult to You
You are so much more than incredible

And for those reasons alone is why
I fell in love with You,
Jesus

Chapter 5

Electric Work

*But they that wait upon the Lord
shall renew their strength;
they shall mount up with wings as eagles;
they shall run, and not be weary;
and they shall walk, and not faint.*

--Isaiah 40:31 KJV

God's electrifying power strengthens us to push through the mazes of life. Though we walk through the valley of the shadow of death, we shall fear no evil.
God is with us wherever we go.

--Psalms 23:4 Paraphrased

Life sometimes leaves circumstances questionable. We do not always understand why certain things happen the way they do. However, we must trust that our Father has everything under control.

God knows better than we do, but we become so arrogant thinking that we are some type of genius. Instead of waiting on God, we take matters into our own slippery hands. Then, we wonder why life gets away from us. Before we know it, our valley-walk gets darker. If only we would get out of our own way and be more like Jesus.

I like how Jesus Christ prayed to Dad when he was deeply distressed and troubled. He said, Abba, Father, all things are possible unto thee; take away this cup from me: *nevertheless not what I will, but what thou wilt.* *Mark 14:36 KJV.*

Like Jesus, surrender self to God. Strive to live Christ: "Your will, not mine!"

Prayer of the Day

Today we will not be bonded by fear
We will answer Your call
We will do exactly what was told by You
We declare change

Oh God, remodel our walk
Make new our tongue
Let us speak with approved words by You
Let us think differently than when we were young

Let us think of more than ourselves
Let us take interest in the need of others
God, give us compassion
Take hate away by allowing love to cover

God let us be united
And not focus on the color of one's skin
The human race has a wide range of diverse complexion
But we're all the same within

We realize You have been too good to us
While we have yet to give You our all
We fall
In the trap of our wicked hearts
And wonder why we are always in the dark

When we are in a bad position in our life,
Let us find the way out, let us seek Your face
In this race
Because You give us the best route

We have allowed the shadow to block the view
Of You
But God we say no more
Today we declare vision of the righteous
Where You are
We will see
We will be
No more would we ignore

The power of Your greatness we do not always understand
But we are too blessed
To not express
Empower us to evangelize and tell our fellow man
About You
In Jesus Name, Amen

Things I Don't Hear Enough Of

I do not hear enough of God's voice
Maybe I choose not to listen
I been lying to myself
Maybe I am a politician

I became deaf to every instrument
That could not make my heart beat
I no longer listen to foolishness
No need to put it on repeat

I do not hear enough truth
From your lips that flows with lies
Give me proof
I cannot let anything fly

I do not hear enough "I love you"
Love words are far beyond my reach
My ears slightly clench
When you get into your emotional speech

I need abundance
I want something greater
I have to change pace now
I cannot wait until later

I do not hear enough respect
Children have no manners
Talking back and confusing their parents
with their poor grammar

I do not hear enough peace
Churches are getting attacked
Kids are in trouble
School shootings back to back

I want to hear more than negativity
I am praying for a positive vibe,
Give me peace
Give me joy
I need a cure that only God can prescribe

I do not hear enough unity
God's people not speaking the same
Religion is division
Messing up what God has proclaimed

I do not hear enough laughter
The devil too busy trying to destroy
I want to see more smiles
Do not allow him to steal your joy

I do not hear enough
The volume has been turned down
I have tuned out everything
That makes unnecessary sound

I want to hear God's voice
Matter of fact I want to listen
I want to hear I love you,
I love you without clenching

I want to hear something
That makes my heart beat
I want God, the truth
So let us go deep

I want to hear more than negativity
I am praying for a positive vibe,
Give me peace
Give me joy
I need a cure that only God can prescribe

Dream on

What do you want to be?
What dream do you see?
Is it so far out of reach
that it becomes discouraging?

Do not doubt
Believe
Do not become too proud to plead
Ask God for the vision,
He will give you sight to see

What do you want to be?
What dream do you see?
Is it so far out of reach
that it becomes discouraging?

Understand you are the dream
The enemy is waiting for the right moment
To block the dream which is you

Meanwhile using tactics to distract
He is a thief in the night trying to destroy you

Be not defeated
Beat the odds
Jump over the obstacles,
Be not discouraged
Encourage yourself
Fade out the world
Because it is disposable

What do you want to be?
What dream do you see?
Is it so far out of reach
that it becomes discouraging?

The Devil wants to stop the dream
He does not want you to succeed
He can care less if you prosper
And get a taste of glory

You are the dream
Open your eyes from the drooling sleep
Wipe the crust from over your eyes
Breathe

Inhale the blessings,
Exhale the failed lessons
That you have vacuumed up from the nostrils
of this world's scenery

God made you a reservation
At the be all you can be
And to be the dream
It takes a lot of preparation

Nightmares deserve cancellation
When you are chosen by God
Things will manifest
Leaving the question in the air
How, did that happen?

But there will be no explanation
All you can say is,
"But God"
He is the artist of all great creations

Dream on
Take ownership of what is before you
Dream on
Let nothing stand in the way of you
Dream on

Believe God will do what He says He will do
God will never leave you nor forsake you

If you put God first
Then everything else will follow
Embrace today
Cannot count on tomorrow

All you have to do is paint the picture
That has already been drawn
Give life color
And Dream on

His Timing

Plans are hopeful
We dream anticipating the day it turns into reality
Making sure every step is taken
Trying to lead the way
Forgetting God is in control of every technicality

Everything you think you may have in check
May not go as planned
We're on God's time
Everything is in His hands

They say, "You shouldn't have a baby after a certain age."
Why give a clock when you are not the one giving time?
People really need to stop and mind their own business

Listen,
Statistics you can dismiss it
Live by the acronym of F.A.I.T.H.
Facts Actually Impelling To Happen

Do not just listen to words
God will show you action

To that mother who tried to conceive and experienced
many complications,
Do not give up
There is a tiny seed inside the womb
God will soon reveal to you
Just be patient

It is hard seeing unfit mothers
popping out children left and right
While that woman who is a perfect fit for an infant
Has yet to experience the visit

Don't you worry though
Your time is coming
You may not know when
But God is up to something

I want you to smile
Close your eyes and your ears if you have to
So you won't be distracted any longer
From the things the enemy tried to steal from you

The time is coming
Where you will be ecstatic
Blessings are coming down
So clear the clutter and make room inside the attic

God wants you to empty the space
So He can take His place
Let Him show Himself to you
And all He can do

When you are finally able to hold your little one,
While gazing into his eyes
Instantly you would recognize
In that moment
It was nobody but God

This Means War

Sometimes I battle with myself
My soul and my flesh
I want to do one thing
My soul says no
But my flesh says yes
It's ok
A little won't hurt you
But my soul says,
A little is just as bad as a lot
If it is unpleasing to God
Then you shall not

I realized it is the enemy who tries to entice us

For we wrestle not against flesh and blood, but against principalities, against powers, against the rulers of the darkness of this world, against spiritual wickedness in high places.
Ephesians 6:12 KJV

We must suit up
Get ready to fight
Dress for the battle
Women, take off the earrings
Man, grab the Vaseline,
I am not talking about petroleum jelly
I am talking about the full armor of the King
Shinning the knees for prayer
To get ready for the war that is going on

When the enemy is facing in my direction
And tries to come close to me,
This means war
When there is an attack on my brothers and sisters in
Christ,
This means war

Division
False prophets
Polished up sins
Acceptance by society
Brain-washing kids
Programming their mind
Only to make their brain another piece of technology

They are no longer thinking on their own

Their processor is being controlled by the enemy
Their software has been attacked with a virus that is
spreading world wide
Only God can fix this chaos
So I make my residence a neighbor to His side

War is going on
The battlefield is crowded
Jammed with hatred
Rage and jealousy
Adultery
Fornication
Homosexuality
The devil is coming so hard to destroy humanity

We must resist the enemy
Tell him,
Get thee behind me, Satan: Matthew.16:23 KJV
I will not stand for brutality

I stand tall as a tree
I sting harder than a bee
God is on my side
No weapons that form against me shall prosper
Isaiah 54:17 Paraphrased
I wear the armor of God

So I am bulletproof
Dodging the missile

The Lord will fight for me
So I shall hold my peace
I have decided to live with God
So I signed a permanent lease

In this war,
I may get struck down
But I will not be destroyed
You may look at me like a dollar bill
But you are a check that is void
You have no value to me
What you offer, I avoid

I stand tall as a tree
I sting harder than a bee
God is on my side
No weapons that form against me shall prosper
Isaiah 54:17 Paraphrased
I wear the armor of God
So I am bulletproof
Dodging the missile

I speak favor over my life

I seek Savior

For He made the ultimate sacrifice

I fight

Because the armor of God is my shield

I am protected

No need to be caution

So I do not yield

I am going all in

I am not afraid of this battlefield

I fight

Not with fist or fright

Not with signs to protest

But with words of prayer

Day and night

Giving me the power to properly fight

Once I get off my knees

There, I stand tall as a tree

I sting harder than a bee

God is on my side

No weapons that form against me shall prosper

Isaiah 54:17 Paraphrased

I wear the armor of God

So I am bulletproof
Dodging the missile

Satan has set up his traps
To capture souls, he can devour
Looking to the weak
Rearing them in with things they desire

Be strong
And stand tall as a tree
Fight for your life
Sting hard as a bee

Remember God is on your side
Just pray
War you will conquer
Because *no weapon that is formed against thee shall*
prosper Isaiah 54:17 Paraphrased

Light Switch

Thy word is a lamp unto my feet,
and a light unto my path. Ps. 119:105 KJV
In a world of darkness
Jesus
You are all I have

Lord,
Supply the supplies I need to live clean
In this dirty world,
Let my light shine
In the lives of every boy and girl

I am stuck in a position
I am all the way up
I am a light switch
That should not be touched

The Lord is my light and my salvation;
whom shall I fear?

The Lord is the strength of my life;
of whom shall I be afraid?
Psalms 27:1 KJV

No one I think
God made me so strong
I break through any barricade,
You cannot invade my parade

The world
They tell me
It is corrupt
Bedraggled
Unclean
Extremely filthy
Filled with evil

But I thought on the very first day
God took away darkness
See, the earth was formless and void
Darkness dressed the surface of the deep
But God was moving over the surface of the waters
He said, *"Let there be light." Genesis 1:3 KJV*

And there it was
A world that was glowing

Brightly beautiful
Magnifying and meaningful
Multiplying and fruitful
The authentic truth

So is it the world that is dirty?
Or, is it me and you?
Putting our hands on the light switch
When we have no business to

Do something to wash the interior
Instead of polishing up the exterior
Souls are eroding
From the bacteria
Polluting the body
Contamination from the media

People confessing their opinions
Others are cosigning
Without looking into the word for the truth
Too busy wrapped in their feelings

Mouths are wide open
Facts are substituted by opinions
Opinions solidify our ignorance
Ignorance is unknowing

Not knowing becomes the comfort zone
We become too lazy to search the scripture
Stupidity we begin to own

We are the ones who turned off the lights
Let us flip the switch back on
For so long
We have lost our way
Now we have blood on our hands
But it is time to clean up
And go back to where we belong

Living clean in a dirty world
Is not always easy
Cannot escape issues
By drowning in the glass of a martini
Instead get lit on the love of Jesus

Let Him shine
For He is the light of the world
Do not get captured by the curse
Let Jesus in
For He is the Savior of the universe

There was darkness
Until the light switch

Do you see Him?
Are your eyes closed shut?
Tightly stitched?
Open your pupils
Hit the light switch

If we all transform into His image
The world would not be classified as dirty
Clean up you
I will wash off me
Just because the world may be sloppy
Does not mean we should be
So do your part
And live clean
In a world of people who are filthy

Too Blessed to Not Express

Right now,
I declare peace in the valley of depression,
In the valley of cancer,
In the valley of bad finances
and disconnected marriages,
In the valley of low self-esteem
and anger that is hard to manage

In the valley of the shadow of death
God,
We shall fear no evil
Because we know You are with us wherever we go,
Psalms 23:4 Paraphrased

Even in the midst of the passing of a loved one
God,
Help us understand that it is just a shadow
Creating fear in our eyes
I declare we will make it through the valley

With praises unto Your sweet Name,
God

See, You get us through the test
So we can see and breathe success
We are way too blessed to not express

Weight is on the chest of the people
Trying to find a balance between the world and You
In ways that is illegal

Claiming holiness
When purity has been sucked up
by the vacuum of demonic conveniences
Sometimes we have to go through something
to be taught something
It is called valley experiences

God,
I must speak to You
911
It is an emergency
Someone needs to be rescued

The tag on their life seems to be hidden
Now they fail to see their value

Losing hope
Cannot cope with their situation
So they do not want to continue

Suicide is on the front line of the battle
Eating off the wrong tree
Death lies inside of the apple

Wrong choices they seem to be making
Someone is walking in the Garden of Eden
Realizing that they are naked
Covering up with leaves that fit their situation
Eyes opened once the serpent revealed
Something that was so sacred

Adoring the butterflies
While dodging the bees
Running and hiding
Trying to find shade under the trees

God please cancel the track meets
No more should we run or hide
We must seek
Even in our darkest hour
Let us praise You
Because You have been too good for us not to see

the fruit You produced

The seeds grew into beautifully flawed women and men
Life began when breath was breathed into the nostrils
Putting spirit inside of the human

Purity diminishes as soon as we take our first breath
The more days we see
The more we crawl and become
a sneaky, slimy, slimy snake
Death and life are in the power of the tongue:
Proverbs18:21 KJV
Using it to build up and break

Generation after generation
Falls into the same hole
Living the story of the family that has already been told
We need to get to the root
To stop the production of producing rotten fruit
Break cycles
Break free from nipples

The world baby us
We are stuck to its breast
Thinking we are getting good nutrition
But actually it is keeping us in the same condition

The clock is in position
Blessings are in sight now
It is all because of God
Praise right now
Nothing is ever too bad to tell somebody how good God is
We are way too blessed to not express
Why not get it off your chest
When you vent about everything else

Some are stuck in the valley
Cannot see the mountain top
Their situation is disturbing their mind
Allowing the shadow to have God blocked

It is nothing but the power of fear
That is holding us back
But LET GO and feel the breeze
In the land of God
Right now, I declare peace

I Lift My Praise

I lift my hands to You
I lift my praise to You
Through every situation
You have been my rescue

My helping hand when I was falling down
You pulled me through every situation
I was at the bottom
But I am at the top now

My view is clearer up here
I can see the ground where I kept falling
And tripping over fear that had me crawling
Trying to get to my safe haven which is You

You have brought me places
There You left me speechless
Words I cannot gather

My vocabulary and my mind is too small
To even begin to fathom the ability to express words
Of how great You are
So instead...

I lift my hands to You
I lift my praise to You
Through every situation
You have been my rescue

My Savior
My Lord
My Creator
My God

You have been more than I can ever ask for
More than I can see
You are my knowledge
Bearing fruit on my tree
You help me grow so beautifully

You delivered me from myself
Anger brought me to a mental suicidal convention
I did not see the reason to live
But You knew the purpose
You saw my value,

When I thought I was worthless

Through my flaws
You give me hope and make me feel gorgeous regardless
This world is a thesaurus
And I am the synonym
Trying to mimic the image of You
I slip up sometimes and live the opposite
I really want to stop it

It is hard when the world strips you apart
Leaving the apparel off to reveal every speckle,
I feel naked
I guess I too should not have eaten the fruit
But it was something about the apple
Caused me to disobey You
Tricked by my own desires
But I threw them in a lake of fire
I repent in the garden
And there...

I lift my hands to You
I lift my praise to You
Through every situation
You have been my rescue

When I think about the day my daddy left me fatherless
I lift my hands to You
When I reminisce about how my mom struggled
To raise six kids
I lift my praise to You
When my grandma ascended to the heavens
In my grievance
You were there
Through every situation
You have been my rescue

When I think about your goodness,
God
I lift my hands to You
When I think about your grace
I lift my praise to You
You are a way-maker,
God
Through every situation
You have been my rescue

Heaven

When I get to heaven
I will shout and make a joyful noise
To know I was a good leader
For the little girls and boys

When I get to heaven,
I will cry blissful tears
To know my work was not in vain
Through all the challenging years

When I get to heaven,
I will laugh because I can, and until it tickles my soul
I will dance as if no one is watching
Because I have met my goal

I will twirl and twirl in my white robe
I will smile and smile
Until my cheeks hurt
Even then I may continue to smile

To know I am living on land that is sweeter than dessert

I will fight a good fight
I will keep my faith in the Lord
Because I know the day will come
When I will receive my reward

When I get to heaven,
I would see what I was missing all along
Heaven is so heavenly
A place,
I can one day call home

Chapter 6

The Black We Paint

Have we not all one father? Hath no one God created us? Why do we deal treacherously every man against his brother, by profaning the covenant of our fathers?

--Malachi 2:10 KJV

Endeavoring to keep the unity of the Spirit in the bond of peace.

--Ephesians 4:3 KJV

The black we paint on the walls of African American souls is a misconception. All the dots have not been connected. For some time now there has been a major disconnection. Even the dictionary and thesaurus define black with unkind words that give the black race a meaning we do not deserve.

When I looked up the word black, synonyms that popped up were dark, hopeless, dirty, angry, and evil. Lastly, it listed African American, in that order. If only I could take some ink removal to those negative words; I would erase and fill the space with strong, powerful, creative, world-builder, and way-maker. Proper terminology that describes me.

Black is hiding 'Colored' folks. God created us all in color. We are all the same just different shades. Our skin tone is irrelevant to God. His focus is on the inward man. Stereotypes formed along the way must be knocked down.

If truth be told, the black we paint of ourselves at times are shameful. When society mistreats one of us, we fall in the trap by striking back in ways unapproved by God. I know it is frustrating to hear we are not good enough by people's loud, consistent wordless acts. However, do not give power to the world and allow its perception to dictate who we are and what we become as black people.

When negativity comes, let us speak God's Word to respond. Do not retaliate with hate. Allow love to be the crime.

No Guns, Just Peace

No guns
No weapons
Just peace

No guns
No weapons
He,
Dr. King stood for justice,
nonviolence and equality

Let us find a balance quickly
Our movements have been slow
Let inspirational words drip from the lips
Instead of all that shade we throw
Let the crooked ground straighten
As the current in the river flow

No guns
No weapons

Just peace

He did not dream for us to sleep
on the destruction of this world
and be blindfolded
From all the things they refused
to put in the textbooks
They did not want us to know

We are still in slavery
Not out in the fields picking cotton
But we are mentally enslaved
We throw away knowledge
The power of our mind, we have forgotten

Do we remember all that Dr. King fought for?
It is a constant reminder that maybe it was a waste
Because some do not want to change a thing
So here is the cotton

Stay right where you are
If you do not want to explore
I cannot force you to move
I am walking to new heights
I have never seen before

I am bringing peace like a river with me
Holding hands with someone who does not look like me
I am bringing justice
I am ready to fight
No guns
No weapons
I will bring my words of God on site
Letting the power of my tongue speak boldly
on what is wrong and right

Our issues should be born into resolution
But yet we keep giving birth to unjust situations
Only to give it up for an adoption
Making our issues someone else's problem
We must stop it

Officers killing black men without being charged
Blacks retaliating
Shooting and hating every cop they lay their closed eyes on
Protesting and do not even know what they are fighting for

What do we stand for?
What do the eyes see?
Is it the color of the skin
that is killing you,
that is killing me?

I wish we were color blind
And focused on what is within
Respect each other as equal
Skin is not the sin

It is time for the violence to cease
No guns
No weapons
Just peace

Most Wanted

It is something about the pigment of your skin
Your complexion brings attraction
Black man,
You are most wanted
You are such a distraction
Got police on the lurk
Itching to come in your direction
Black man,
I am tired of seeing so many of you absent

Gunned down and killed by officers
Gunned down by another black man
Controlled by Lucifer
Black man
Take a stand
No longer be silenced
What's going on is not right
So much is off balanced

Destruction of the world leaves everything damaged
Back away from the submission
And step to the challenge

You are most wanted to not succeed
To be locked in jail
And abandon your breed

You are most wanted
To be chained to the street
So the hungry law can pick you up
You are the perfect plate for them to eat

It is something about the pigment of your skin
Your complexion brings attraction
Black man,
You are most wanted
You are such a distraction
Got police on the lurk
Itching to come in your direction
Black man,
I am tired of seeing so many of you absent

They are taking our sons
Our brothers

Our fathers
Our husbands

We are taking our sons
Our brothers
Our fathers
Our husbands

We are not focused on us
We are pointing fingers at them
Either way it is a life lost
Now a black child with a father
Chances are even slim

Black people,
We are under attack
Not just by whites, but also with blacks
Help me to figure out
What is wrong with that?

So many crimes attempt
We do not want white hands on us
But black on black crime should not be exempt
All must end

It is something about the pigment of your skin

Your complexion brings attraction
Black man,
You are most wanted
You are such a distraction
Got police on the lurk
Itching to come in your direction
Black man,
I am tired of seeing so many of you absent

I see him on the billboard
A model for the crime scene
Advertising guilt
When guilty is not he

An innocent black man
Forced to take an unfair deal,
Where he pleads guilty
Just so he can get a lesser sentence
For a crime he never committed

He was only guilty for one thing
And that was being chocolate
Black, brown, or whatever you want to call it

My uncle was a target
One night as he was walking

He fit the description of who the officers were looking for
A black man wearing white and black tennis shoes
Really?....
Confused?
Amused?
Because the description was so vague
How many people
have white and black tennis shoes these days?

He was just a black man
At the wrong place
At the wrong time
So jail he faced
10 months
Only to say it was a mistake

I tell ya
It is something about the pigment of your skin
Your complexion brings attraction
Black man,
You are most wanted
You are such a distraction

Got police on the lurk
Itching to come in your direction
Black man,

I am tired of seeing so many of you absent

Do not retaliate with weapons
It only makes matters worse
Guns end lives
React once you think first

Do not take another man's life
Just because you are treated unfair
Justice will be served
All you have to do
Is go to God in prayer

Letter To My Black Brotha

Dear black brotha,
I know it was not easy
Being raised in a household with a single mother

Daddy was not there to teach you how to be a man
He left you to figure it out
You did the best you can

I see your struggles
As you try to find all the pieces to the puzzle
There is a constant rain
Life you juggle
When it floods
Restrain from drowning
You gotta swim out the puddles

Every day is a wakeup call
Do you rise to the alarm?
Or, do you press snooze?

because sleeping is the norm?

My black brotha
It is time to get up
Night has come and gone
It is a new day
Start to see the light as if it is dawn

God created you with a distinct purpose
Apparently, distraction is happening all around you
But you gotta stay focused

Do not buy into the lies
Find your purpose
Know you are a product of God
Already been Purchased!

You just have not accepted it yet
Maybe you do not think you are worthy
from all those mess ups
Just, Thank God
Lord have Mercy!

It is time to walk in destiny
You been feeding yourself off the devalue meal
way too long

It is time to intake a new recipe

It seems you got stuck in an environment
Where the people do not jump
When there is a positive opportunity
Don't you want to be a leader for the ones without drive?
I mean, somebody gotta be strong enough
To move the community

Your name is penciled on a jail cell
But you're the only one who can erase it
You choose who you want to be
We all have a dream, but we all don't chase it

Lens are blurry
You are losing focus
Cannot snap the shot when it is too much motion
It is time to be still
Instead of being a part of the commotion

This letter I wrote,
Hoping it would reach
Learn something
So you can go out and teach

Daddy has failed you

Your community has too
Law enforcement sometime drops the ball
But if you do your part
You would not have to worry at all

Your experiences do not define you
The past is old news
Today, you can do something different
You just have to choose!

1619

When are we going to start reading?
Why are we keeping our mind way back in 1619,
when slavery was born in America?
The day a ship
Brought 20 African slaves ashore
to the British colony of Jamestown, Virginia

It amazes me
How history
Repeats itself like lies
That's been told
So many times
Until it becomes someone's truth

Slave owners
That prohibited
our ancestors from reading and writing
Do not need
To have a hold on you

But somehow lies slip into our reality

When we fall
We are quick to reach
For something to grab on
We have held on to
That slave mentality
Fear has connected
To our personality

Bondage keeps us from being free
Sometimes we can be our own slave owner
Restraining ourselves from victory
Why not create a new story
that can one day give color
to black history?

Same old cycle
It is a heavy load
But we have to wash and dry
Before we can fold
We rather tuck things away
Than cleaning it up
We have limited ourselves
Our mind we corrupt
Hold up

We are so busy
Protesting Black Lives Matter
But we are not polishing our own black
So to whom does it matter?
We are bowing down
To ignorance
It has become our master

We turn our back
Eyes behind our head
Focusing on things of the past
Let us march forward instead

1619
Should be a memorable year
That motivates us
To have no fear
Fear has been blocking
our vision
From the beginning
Scarred
By every whipping

Those whips
Look at it with pride
Because every lick

Left a mark
A representation
Of your strength
lies at the core
Of your foundation

Everything
Is not what it seems
Let us vow
To never relive 1619

Let us reach
For a book
Just because we can
We're at the end
Of this phenomenon
Let us take a stand

Applaud
Every person
That told us we can't
For they make us stronger
To lift up our voice and tell them,
"Yes we can!"

I am guilty
Of being trapped in the "No"
I must escape to the "yes"
Follow me
Because I am following the Teacher
He is the best

Life is filled
With a load of assessments
So stay ready for the test
Open your book
Read for you
I suggest
"Do you!"
Do not worry about the rest

Chapter 7

Living 2 Comfortable

No man can serve two masters:
for either he will hate the one,
and love the other;
or else he will hold to the one
and despise the other.
Ye cannot serve God and mammon.

--Matthew 6:24 KJV

M ost people want it all. Serving God and living our way is so convenient and comfortable. It puts us in danger. God wants us to take the necessary way in. It is impossible to be at two places at the same time. Either we are here or there, in or out, with God or against Him.

Never get comfortable living a double life. The Bible states, *Because thou art lukewarm, and neither cold nor hot, I will spue thee out my mouth. Revelations 3:16 KJV*

Personally, I do not want God to spit me out nor say He never knew me. When my work is done on earth, I want Our Father to say," *Well done, good and faithful servant; thou hast been faithful over a few things, I will make thee ruler over many things:" Matthew 25:23 KJV*

Criminal Hands

Blood was on my hands from the crime scene
Death was staring me in the face from the poison that went
up my bloodstream
I became a murderer within seconds of breathing
I did not live long
I instantly began dying
Marinating in sin
Just called me iniquity

My criminal hands
I tried to wash the gun residue off
But it kept on lingering
And reminding me of what I had done

The words from my tongue
Brought so many people to the grave scene
Hurt people, hurt people
It does not make anything better
I was still hurting

Tired of the pain
So I had to adjust some things
Got on my knees and started praying
"Our Father who art in heaven,
Hallowed be thy name. Thy kingdom come.
Thy will be done in earth, as it is in heaven."
Matthew 6: 9-10
I am on my knees here to make my confession

All these days
I worked as a sinner
Did not think about day number seven where I rest
Sleep to dream on making life better
Now I rest

Older now
Judgment day keeps poking my brain
The words, I never knew you
Just do not seem the same
as well done my good and faithful servant
So getting my life right with You,
God is priority
Number urgent
All action no words need to be spoken
All along
I have been cleaning my clothes with bad detergent

So I went down in the watery grave of baptism
To wash this dirt off me
I was tired of looking like a serpent

Did not speak the language of the Bible
Now, I see it is important
This language barrier causes me to be ruined
So it is time to become fluent

On my own words, I started choking
I stopped the jokes
Because I see you were not laughing
So I know you ain't joking

Criminal hands
Dripped in blood
Leading people astray
To drown in the flood

Our truth is not accurate
It is more like our personal desires
The truth has been twisted
So just call us some liars

Our truth is whatever we believe it to be
The truth is looked all over

Like it is some kind of mystery

God is the truth
Cleaning the residue
From our criminal hands
That has been in everybody's business

Putting our two cents in
Like we can afford it
We do more damage than good
Like we can afford it
If we cannot back up our opinions with scripture
There is no need to support it
There is so much blood on the hands of the people
And they don't even know it

Accepted things of the world
And trying to get others to feel comfortable in the change
We must watch the seeds we plant
Some things do not grow as planned

Homicide

Is it really homicide?
Is that what you tell yourself
so it would not look like suicide?

You can remember the crime scene as if it was yesterday
Someone damaged your childhood
Scarred you for life
On the inside, you started backing away

Homicide is how it was identified
Death was justified by every excuse
You did not want to feel guilty
So you covered up the truth
With thick sheets of anything that would warm you

She

He

Holds on to pain from yesterday
Build soundproof walls to keep every vibrato out

That tries to shake
Her, Him
Them

Walking barefooted on cracked concrete
Leaving cuts
Deeper than the eyes can see

Is it really homicide?
Is that what you tell yourself for the reason
you are dying?
Your reactions cannot be justified by pointing fingers at
everyone else
Just so it would not look like suicide

Your problems are your own
So discover solutions
Find a solid ground to walk on

Your face is blue
All the air has been sucked up
Because you refused to breathe
You did not want to let go
You continued to squeeze

You are dying
There is nothing left for me to do
I tried everything in my power
Yet, I kept losing

You are not the victim
You were involved in this murder
You would not see tomorrow
Because you allowed yesterday
To escape into today
To borrow your happiness

The reason things do not feel ok
Is because you strayed away
God gave you a life that is vibrant
But you helped turn it gray

You never lived
Death kept taking over your body
You refused to forgive
It is time to make a choice
You must choose to live

The Weak-end

Stepping to God in her old, broken-down stilettos
In need of a high healing
Torn to pieces
Trying to find her absent father
In every man that she encounters

Believing the "I love you"
The: "I am not the average guy"
"Girl I am different"
"You are insecure"
"I am not cheating"
"So stop tripping"
"I am loyal"
"I keep it 100"

But know that only means,
He will tell you what you want to hear
He fears
To tell you the whole truth

Because you cannot handle the real
Well at least that is what he says
The truth shall make you free. John 8:32 KJV
It gives you options
Once you know the truth
You have a choice to deal with it or not
But a lie keeps you caged
Maybe he is afraid
That you will turn the tables
And do unto him as he has done unto you
Giving false truth

All throughout the week
She beats herself down
Strength is nowhere to be found

She is exhausted
Acting as if it is not pretend
Fronting as if everything is cool when she is around others
Anticipating for the weak-end

She is a fragile woman
with a plate piled of unwanted calories
She gains weight from the unhealthy things
she ate from the buffet of the world
Overwhelmed with the excessive collage in her gallery

Pictures that remind her of every mistake
She has ever made
On every picture was a different face
Caked in beauty products
Trying to find her self-esteem,
On the shelf of a cosmetic store
Because someone told her beauty lies
On the cover of a magazine

Enough is enough
She is fed up
So long she allowed everyone else
To define her with their opinions
But she began to seek God for her true definition

If you look out a different eye
You will get a different view
Understand everyone may not comprehend the meaning of you

As long as you know your worth
You will clearly see your value
If you want to see what is in store
Seek God and He will show you a preview

There she goes
Broken and tired of the drama in her life

Tired of feeling worthless
Tired of feeling incapable of victory
Tired of giving up
In need of strength
Drained with weakness
She is in need of energy

Watching the clock
Wishing to turn the hands of time
To the moment this will be over

Hands in the air
The old fight has ended
Her fight is now different
She surrenders and starts over
Joined the army of God
To become a true soldier

The weak must end
Sin is beneath the gravity that pulls us down
But yet we tend to level with the ground
To get comfortable

Yet we toss and turn all day long
Iniquity makes us so dizzy
We stand with hands over our eyes

Fighting to clear our minds
And see what's right in front of us

Thank God for Jesus
Thank Jesus for His blood,
His death and resurrection
Because of Him we live
And should not give the world
The satisfaction of gaining our soul

Lies been told
But yet we accept the stories
Yes God loves you
But He hates sin
If you are not all in
And all you do is doubt
You are lukewarm to Him
And He will spit you out

Poetry Is

Poetry is my life
The air I breathe
The lungs
The arms
The sleeves
The joy I squeeze
Holding tight to the art
Splitting my spirit and flesh apart
So I can clearly understand the operation of God
When I am on that road I sometimes plod

Poetry is
Gorgeous
Creative
Harmless
A way to be free
Unique
Different it sees

Poetry is outspoken
Heart wide open
Expression of feeling
Style and rhythm
Rhythm and blues
Exposed lies to show what is true
Poetry illustrates that there is more depth to me and you

Poetry is deep
Painting beautiful words
Leaving the mind to imagine the creative masterpiece

If Jesus Was Never Born

I am into the art of life
Intrigued by the creation of man
And how even one child can be temporarily placed
Inside of a woman
Leaving a bond of a life time

But the most fascinating birth I have ever heard of
Was the birth of Jesus
Born of a virgin
Just to come save us

A carnal mind cannot envision this conception
Their mind tells them a man had to be involved in the connection
Maybe that is why so many do not believe in Christ
Because his life was formed inside the womb of Mary
By the Holy Spirit
Joseph, her significant other wanted to split
Until an angel of the Lord made a visit

What if Jesus was never born,
and it was totally up to us to save ourselves?
How many of us would make it
with our "all about me" attitudes
and all the "I don't cares?"

If Jesus was never born,
who else would be there
when your friends turn their back on you?
Or, your family becomes distant
the very minute you stop allowing them to use you
when you finally request your money back?

You remember that time they borrowed it
three, four months ago?
Now, they are holding on to feelings
and refuse to let go
Who else will be there?

In the valley,
When everything seems dark
And the cancer holds your life in its hands
In that time
The mountain seems too high to climb
Who will be your healer?

If Jesus was never born,
Would the blind man have been able to see?
Would the leper have been cured from his leprosy?
Some are living as if the birth of Jesus has never occurred
They are blinded by words that has no actions
Listening to that little bird
Holding those useless words higher than the gospel

It is sad
And they really do not want to hear that
But I am like Paul the apostle,
*"Am I therefore become your enemy, because I tell you the
truth." Galatians 4:16 KJV*

The truth shall make you free John 8:32 KJV
There is no need to beef
We must get along
Be strong
And stick close to the Son of Man, who was born to save us
God knew we would be too weak on our own
So He gave us Jesus
Who bled and died on the cross

From His birth and death
We die into life
Where the gates of heaven will open wide

And we will finally meet Christ

Face to face with Him
I become apologetic
Ashamed
Because sometimes my walk with Him was slightly synthetic

I been convicted
I am guilty
I feel I have crucified our Lord
And kept Him on the cross every time I sinned

My head has fallen down in shame
To know I had part in the pain
Because of the way I was living
But I am given a second chance
From His birth
His death
We are forgiven

Pimping God

If Jesus wore a tight shirt that showed off his muscles
Or a short skirt if He was in the form of a woman
Will you then lay eyes on Him?
Will you then long for conversation?
Intrigued by every word
that flows from the tip of His tongue to the outward part of
His lips
Will you then hear Him?

If He was popular on BET or VH1
OWN, Lifetime, TV1
Facebook or Twitter,
Will you then watch His heart break
because no one wants to follow Him?
Then, will you follow Him?

Will you then turn the channel of your life?
Not only observing Him on worldly holidays,
But observing Him with a daily celebration for His sacrifice?

If He got turnt up from that unpleasant sound we call music,
Then, will you get down with Him?
If He treated you like that dude that cares nothing about you
But yet still wants to have sex with you,
Will you then desire intimacy with Him?
We must do some self-evaluation

Father,
I am going to take out the time right now
To apologize for Your dysfunctional children,
Who refuses to serve You, when you reject their leftovers
Giving You the crumbs when You just blessed them a million

They are so used to artificial
That when something as real as You come to their face
They cannot recognize what it is
Do not know how true love feels

It seems they like to get gyp
So, I guess they want You to rip out
what is right underneath them

Their environment told them they are worthless
They have no value
They serve no purpose
I am sorry You were never chosen

It is something how a good man always gets looked over
They say, "You are boring"
The Bible is way too planned
Every aspect of life should be instantaneous
It is not special if it is not spontaneous
That is what they believe

I would hate for You to show them how spontaneous
You can get
Taking breath to the funeral
Taking life to the grave
Make them quickly understand,
If they keep taking walks to the shadows of death
It will leave them dead

Jesus,
I am sorry
That the people You died for
Do not even respect Your stripes
They are living murderers
To Your back they twist the knife
And piercing Your side to take Your life

Unspoken conviction
Bringing You to Calvary
To relive the Crucifixion

So many do not believe in You
So they do not follow
Bible verses they swallow
Digest only what is convenient
One minute they agree with the Word
The next minute they do not
Change is so frequent

Living for today
Without thinking about tomorrow
Do not want to buy Your Word
They just want to borrow
We live in a world of convenience
Joy is forced to be the twin of sorrow
Identical is just a chemical that makes the judgment
Of the eye so difficult
We put our main focus on the sight
We view out of our peripheral

Things that may look exactly alike
Does not mean it is the same
Unique is the difference
That will always remain

After all You did,
It seems like it still isn't good enough

I can only imagine how You feel
They act so tough
Pronounce them dead and see if they can rise up

Obviously, they are more powerful than You
See, only thing they can resurrect is lies
Clearly won't rise up in the truth

What will it take for you to long for Jesus?
Maybe if He was in a tight shirt
that showed off his muscles?
Or, a short skirt if He was in the form of a woman?
Maybe then you will lay eyes on Him?
If He was popular on BET or VH1
OWN, Lifetime, TV1
FACEBOOK or Twitter,
Maybe then you will follow Him?
If He got turnt up from that unpleasant sound, we call music
Maybe then you will get down with Him?
If He treated you like that dude that cares nothing about you
But yet
Still wants to have sex with you
Maybe then you will desire intimacy with Him?

Do you really want the truth?
Or, you want to believe true falsification?

Do you really want God?

Or, is He just another personification

symbolizing that object you desire to use?

God you substitute

Only looking for what you can get

Pimping God

Like He is a prostitute

Giving Him less than 10 percent

As if He has left you hanging before

And has done nothing for you

Let me ask you a question,

What is wrong with you?

Doubting Thomas

I am just a Christian trying to make it
I sin daily just like everyone else
No need to even fake it
For what
For who
God knows the truth

I am so tired of you
Devil dressed in a Christian suit
Lying up the truth as if it is linen on the kitchen table
Getting ready for the false menu
It is so transparent
That when you hold it up
I can see right through you

Church is becoming a group of men with weave
Cannot be the head if you cannot lead
Excuse me please
Do not get it twisted

When I say men with weave
I am not talking about men who be twisting
Not calling no one gay
Just saying some are fake
Why act like "Christians?"

In the building
Praising and worshiping
so hard that you put your back out of place,
at the end of each service
Agreeing to everything the preacher is saying
While sweeping your mess underneath the surface

I am so tired of you
I am talking to those who cannot let go of what someone
did four, five years ago
Bringing up their yesterday's dirt seems to be a perk
It is sad because the highlight of your day
is to see someone hurt

Your lips should be laced
Death is dancing all over your tongue
You have expensive taste
You dress to kill like it is luxury
No one should go through pain after the recovery

I am not perfect
I am a wall of art with a bit of graffiti
Yes I glut
You can find me right there next to greedy
I cannot help it
It seems I can never get enough
It is not my fault
I have a huge appetite for Jesus

My past is not fully behind me
It is an uninvited visitor
Reminding me of hell
Like I do not already get the picture

In the storm,
I look out the windowpane
Hoping to see the clouds of blessings
Coming through the frame
I believe things will get better
The sun must come after the rain

I will not give up
But to be honest,
Sometimes I feel like throwing my hands up
Overwhelmed with the pressure
Driving me nuts

I feel I have a calling on me
That is bigger than my thoughts

I do not want to fail You God
So, I give it to You
For You I trust
I thank You for the art
Even though it is hard sometimes
Standing in front of unfamiliar faces
Pouring out my heart

That tells me I am not doing this for me
I am doing this for You, God
If it was up to me
I will complete incomplete prophecies
You make it possible for me to speak prophetic words
Now they call me poet prophetess

They say I preach
My words are deep
But I know
I have to get deeper into the Word
I do not require a title
I label myself with action
Just call me a verb
The world I send to voicemail

Tell them please do not disturb
I am in focus mode
Ripping up yesterday's paper
Because that news is old

Today is filled with all kinds of matter
Sins are getting fatter
Christians are refusing to drop to their knees
To pray to You,
Master

The church has its mask on
Disguising
Camouflage
Using the gospel for everything, obscuring the truth
Facade
Looking like everything
Walking the earth with their mask on
God use me to take the lost people
And bring them along to Zion

I will be the one to introduce
With the proper introduction
Starting by asking them the million-dollar question
Do you believe Jesus is the son of the living God?
If the answer is no,

We need to have a whole other discussion

He is coming back
How do you not see?
Maybe you need Him to heal your blindness or cure that
leprosy
Obviously, you are sick
and going through an inner body tragedy

I guess you won't believe until you see and touch the holes
in his hands
Not to be smart
I am just saying
Just being honest
Huh, Thomas?

One day you will believe
He is the Son, the Great I Am,
Who gave His life for you to breathe
One day you will no longer fake
You will do exactly what it takes to get to the holy place
You will separate from the world one day
And only desire God
I pray

Judgment Day

(Man)
I have nothing to worry about
I have no fear
Death has come
Judgment Day is here
I know I am saved
All I had to do was confess with my mouth
Believe in my heart
God raised Jesus from the dead
Right?

(Lord)
Wrong...
That was never all
See, that's what is wrong with you Christians
Take a scripture or two that benefits you,
But never thought to look at any more of my word
You are so stuck on Romans chapter 10 verse 9
Child please

I never said that was all
Did you ever for a moment think
to read a little bit further to verse 17?
You must hear the word, in order to believe
If you scroll through the Bible
It also tells you
You must repent, confess, and be baptized
There is so much more scripture I asked you to live by

(Man)
But I...
I thought

(Lord)
But you thought wrong
So into your flesh that you could not clearly see my Spirit
I wanted you to kill that old man that followed the world
and become new
You did not repent like I asked you to
Instead you lied to me
You are nothing but lip with no action
Instead of adding people to my kingdom
You practice mostly subtraction
You did not believe in me
If you did you would have never taken matters
into your own hands

You did not have faith
If so, you would have followed the path I told you to take
You did not love me
You were only interested in the ones
who allowed you to infiltrate
You wanted to be the head
Putting me in the background
What world did you create?

(Man)
But it was not like that

(Lord)
Oh yes it was
You think I am stupid
You want to say you believe, but live your life any kind of way
This is not how this operates
So you know what you deserve right?

(Man)
Why are You doing this?
Lord, Lord have we not prophesied in thy name?
And in thy name have cast out devils?
And in thy name have done many wonderful works?
Matthew 7:22 KJV

(Lord)
Just because you said Lord, Lord does not mean you will
Enter the kingdom of heaven
You all have not done the will of my Father
While you were there on Earth
You allow Facebook to control the likes of you
Twitter you followed
Instagram gave you the perfect picture
Of what seemed popular

The world you put on a pedestal
Looking down on Me
Did you forget?
Man did not die on the cross for your behind to live
That was Me

My Father gave his only Son
But yet that was not enough
Nothing is ever good enough for you
You people are ungrateful
Blind as can be
Here it is
Judgment Day
Now I hear sounds of my Name

Oh now you know me
But it is far too late
You should have seen my value
Instead you spit out all the words I told you,
You should have ate

Time is past due
So depart from me
Ye that work iniquity
I never knew you.
Matthew 7:23 KJV

What's Your Marital Status With God?

Are you single? Or, are you married?

Before you answer,
Let me elaborate
Married is a past single person who chose to collaborate
With another person to elevate

I guess a single person is an un-elevated individual
Who likes to ride solo
Doing everything they want because
they live by the acronym YOLO
Married folks know "You Only Live Once..." though,
They find that One who will help them make it through
Those hard times ain't really hard to find
They draw to the One who can ease their mind

They understand they cannot make it on their own
They cannot do what they want to just because they are "grown"

Obedience is a command that takes away an option
Redemption takes us in
It is part of the adoption

Are you single? Or, are you married to God?
When you are single you get to do you
But marriage is a crucifixion killing the old to become new
Single people do not have to worry
About anyone telling them what to do
They do not care about committing a sin or two

Single people cheat on their husband and wife
Single people see adultery just being a part of life
Single people do not care about messing up a house
Single people pop out kids to trap someone
who is not their spouse

Single people will justify their mistakes
Single people do not show love they rather display hate

Are you single? Or, are you married?

God wants to know,
Are you all in?
Where the relationship stands?
Is it complicated?

Is this love truly activated?
If so, then give God your hand

Trust Him completely
The past we must let go
Remember ye not the former things,
neither consider the things of old. Isaiah 43:18
God gives us favor
Washes away our sins

We do not have to pay for it even though we should,
But Jesus died for us
The ultimate receipt showing it was paid in full

He said, *"It is finished." John 19:30*
But, are you quite done
living life your way,
instead of following the Son?

You tried it your way
Living the single life
Got caught in some things
And probably still paying the price

You tried "everything." Huh?
But how many times have you failed?

Try Jesus
And watch how quickly
He will resurrect you out that hell

God does not want to be friends with benefits
He wants a serious commitment
Give Him your time
More than two minutes

He desires your company
Book your ticket
Through prayer
Go ahead and visit

The bridegroom's marriage has come
Are you the ready bride?
The chosen one?
Are you throwing up your hands because
you are completely done?

I hope not because God wants us all to win
So do not run,
Soon God will reveal the true confirmation
To inform who has won

Remember this:

Every day we are being built. There will be experiences in our lives that we will not understand. Life takes us on journeys where we tour some highs and some lows. Through the good days and the bad, just call on God. He understands what we do not know.

When God is remodeling, He has to demolish some old things in our lives in order to make us brand new. At times, we need a little tweaking. We do not always see when our foundation is sinking, when our paint is chipping, and when those thick walls we put up stop us from inviting others in. God does. He sees that we need new doors because the old ones are stuck closed. He fixes it to where our doors will open. We must walk through.

Many times we make life all about us by sucking up all the air and not allowing for proper circulation. We must learn to think of others more than ourselves.

If we are not compassionate people, we should ask God to give us more compassion.

*If we step outside of ourselves
and let God's will be done,*

All things are possible!

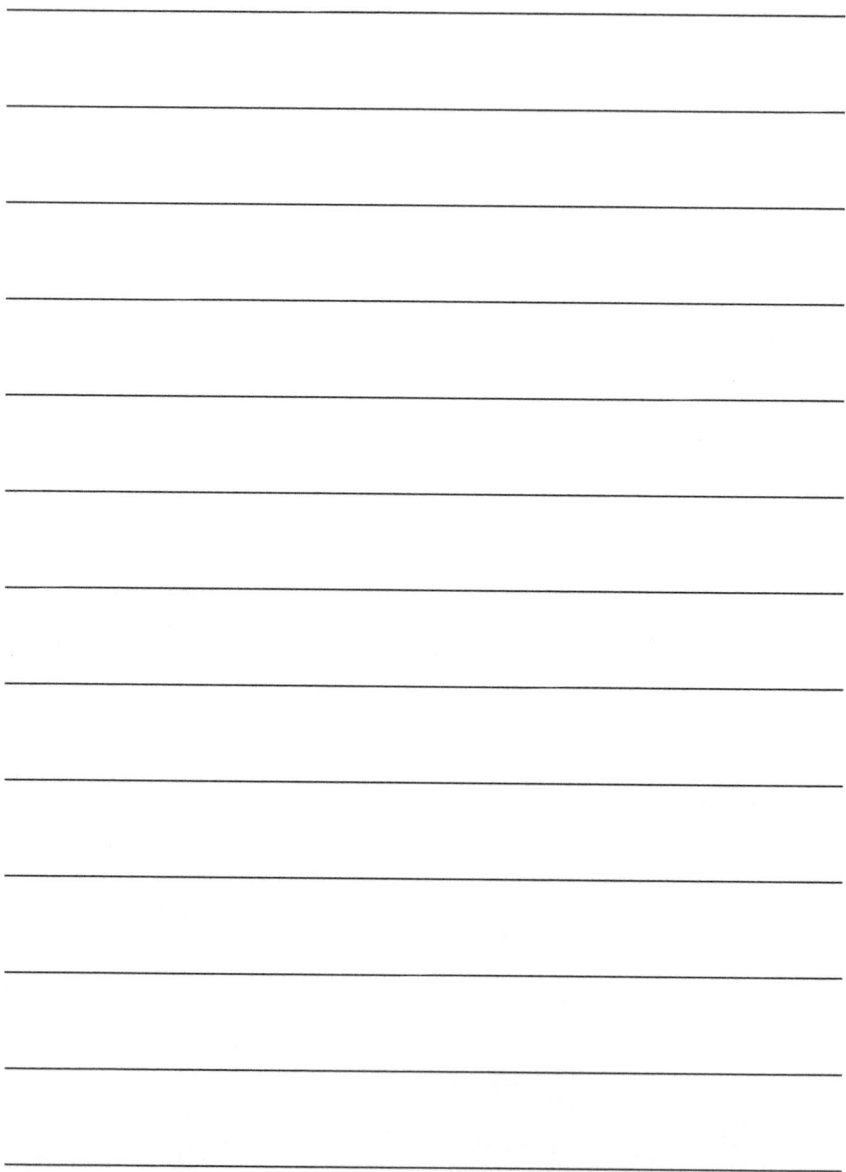

www.ingramcontent.com/pod-product-compliance
Lightning Source LLC
Chambersburg PA
CBHW051952090426
42741CB00008B/1362